THE BROOKLYN SLEUTH

The Police of New York City

robert l. bryan

Published by robert l. bryan, 2023.

THE BROOKLYN SLEUTH

First edition. July 26, 2023.

Copyright © 2023 robert l. bryan.

ISBN: 979-8223191469

Written by robert l. bryan.

For Meghan - the angel on my shoulder.

INTRODUCTION

Detectives have captured the public's imagination for many decades through their exceptional investigative skills, sharp intellect, and unwavering determination to solve complex mysteries. Sherlock Holmes is undoubtedly one of the most iconic detectives in history. This fictional sleuth, created by Sir Arthur Conan Doyle in 1887 was known for his impeccable powers of observation and deductive reasoning. His adventures, chronicled by his loyal friend Dr. John Watson, showcase his brilliance in solving perplexing crimes using his remarkable analytical skills.

Detectives did not attain fame solely through their investigative abilities. It was his good natured, bumbling nature that transported Inspector Jacques Clouseau to fame as the Pink Panther.

Detective fame was not restricted to adults. Since 1930, beloved teenage detective Nancy Drew has been captivating young readers with her remarkable bravery and keen intelligence in solving countless mysteries in her hometown of River Heights.

A detective, however, is not just a character in fiction. Real-life detectives have made significant contributions to the field of criminal investigation, utilizing their skills, experience, and determination to solve complex cases and bring criminals to justice.

Eugene Francois Vidocq, a French criminal-turned-detective, is widely regarded as the father of modern criminal investigation. Vidocq's extensive knowledge of the criminal underworld, disguise skills, and innovative investigative methods helped shape the field of forensic science. He established the first known detective agency in 1817, and his fame was so extensive throughout the 19th century, that it was common for the newspapers to refer to a detective as a "Vidocq."

Scottish born detective Allan Pinkerton is known as the father of American Private Detective Agencies. In the mid-19th century, Pinkerton formed the Pinkerton National Detective Agency, pioneering many investigative techniques still used today. His agency played a crucial role in solving numerous high-profile cases, including foiling assassination attempts on President Abraham Lincoln.

Then there was Brooklyn Police Detective George V. Zundt – George Zundt? Who the heck is George Zundt? George Zundt is the greatest detective no one ever heard of. But now you, dear reader, will learn all about the fascinating story of George Zundt.

CHAPTER 1: POLICING IN BROOKLYN

Before delving into the world of George Zundt, we must first touch on the world of policing in Brooklyn during the 19th century. Brooklyn did not become a famous borough in New York City until 1898. Prior to this consolidation, Brooklyn was an independent city with its own police department.

The first record of Brooklyn being protected by anything that bore a resemblance to a police force was way back in 1669, when Constable Michael Lenell was the sole and only protector of the land. Constable Lenell's duties included whipping and punishing offenders, raising the "hue and cry" after murderers, thieves, robbers, and burglars, to apprehend without warrant such as were overtaken by drink, swearers, sabbath breakers, vagrant persons or night walkers, and then to keep in safe custody until opportunity served to bring them before a justice of the peace for examination.

The first elected police officers were called "Leatherheads" for the hats they wore. It was said that these fellows could sense danger from far off and crawl under their stoops until it was over. In these times, everybody knew each other, so it was presumed that few arrests were made, because a constable who did apprehend a law breaker quickly gained the ill will of everyone else in the village.

Things went on this way for many years, and in 1834 Brooklyn became a full-fledged city with George Hall as mayor. Law enforcement in the city was performed by marshals. Samuel Doxey had the title of First Marshal, and he was assisted by six other marshals working under him. A year later Samuel Vunck was appointed Head Police Officer, while Doxey retained his position as First Marshal. There was also at this time a body of night watchmen who were on duty from sunset to sunrise. [1]

Strangely, when Brooklyn became an actual city there was no provision made for a police department. The new municipal authorities saved themselves the trouble of establishing a police force by appointing more watchmen and recommending that citizens hire their own private security.[2]

In 1850 the State Legislature passed an act providing for the election of a Chief of the Municipal Police and several police captains. The department was organized in the image of the New York Police Department with a superintendent as the chief of police. John Folk was the first superintendent of the Brooklyn Police Department.

In 1859 the Metropolitan Police Act became law in New York State, establishing a police district that stripped the Brooklyn Police Department of its independence. The district comprised the counties of New York, Kings (Brooklyn), Richmond, and Westchester. Up to this time the members of the police force in New York and Brooklyn had been controlled by the local authorities, but now five commissioners were appointed together with the Mayors of New York and Brooklyn to control the police affairs of the four counties.[3]

On April 5, 1870, the State Legislature passed a bill abolishing the Metropolitan Police Act, making the police department in the City of Brooklyn an independent organization. Prior to the 1870s Brooklyn was known as the "City of Homes." What little business it did was supplied by retail stores, breweries, and a few factories. The crowding of Manhattan soon drew attention to the low rents and superb accommodations of its sparsely populated neighbor. Building was done on a large scale, with factories, warehouses, and wholesalers springing up all along the extended waterfront and the banks of Newtown Creek and the Gowanus Canal. The increase in commercial activity was accompanied by a corresponding increase in crime. An increased workload was thrust upon the police department. [4]

In 1898 it was all over when Brooklyn became a borough in the Greater New York City and the Brooklyn Police Department was absorbed into the New York City Police Department.

CHAPTER 2: THE SUPPORTING CAST

Throughout his 24-year career, George Zundt worked closely with hundreds of members of the police department, but three men, in particular, had a profound impact on Zundt's career, and are prominently mentioned in this book. Patrick Campbell was superintendent of the police department throughout almost Zundt's career, and George Waddy and John Mackellar were in charge of the detectives during Zundt's tenure with the detective division. These three men rate a few introductory paragraphs of their own.

Patrick Campbell was born in 1827 in the city of Charleston, South Carolina, but when he was quite young his parents moved to Brooklyn. He secured employment in the office of the Brooklyn Daily Eagle, beginning at the bottom of the ladder. He worked his way up to become the foreman of the Eagle composing room. Very early in life he began to take interest in politics. He became a man of influence and during the administration of President Pierce his services were rewarded by an appointment as Inspector of Customs. In 1866 he was elected by the Democratic Party Sheriff of Kings County. In 1870 Brooklyn abolished the Metropolitan System for its police force and Campbell was made Chief of Police for its independent force. A change in the city charter abolished the office, and on August 12, 1875, he was appointed Superintendent of Police. From the first hour he assumed command of the force he was animated by one idea – efficiency within the department. Before his administration, Brooklyn was infested with gangs and thieves, many who made regular raids from New York. As the executive head of the department the superintendent did much toward increasing the efficiency of the detective corps. There were many men with more detective ability than Campbell, but none with more dogged perseverance. Campbell retired in 1895 and died in 1908.

John Mackellar was born in the old city of New York, of Scottish parents, on May 4, 1843, and when he was two years old his parents moved to Brooklyn In July 1863, Mackellar enlisted in the special force organized to put down the draft riots in New York City. He was on duty day and night during the week of the rioting and received his fair share of hard knocks. When the trouble was over, he was transferred to the Atlantic Dock Squad, a body of men organized to protect property and storehouses in South Brooklyn. In June 1864 Mackellar was made a regular patrolman and six months later he was promoted to sergeant. In 1872 he was promoted to captain and ten years later he was advanced to the rank of inspector.

Mackellar was not the typical looking cop of the era. While many in the department tended to be large of girth and slow of movement, Mackellar was tall, slim, and could sprint faster than the nimblest member of any gang. Out of uniform, he could have been taken for a prosperous business man rather than a member of Brooklyn's "blue and brass" brigade.

When Patrick Campbell retired in 1895 it was generally supposed that Mackellar would be appointed superintendent, but William McKelvey received the appointment, although he had only been an inspector for a short time. By an act of the Legislature the position of deputy superintendent was created, and Mackellar received the appointment. When McKelvey retired, Mackellar was appointed Superintendent of the Brooklyn Police department in 1897. His position only lasted a few months, however. When Brooklyn was consolidated into the Greater City of New York, Mackellar was placed in charge of the Brooklyn force at the rank of deputy chief.

On December 5, 1900, Mackellar left Brooklyn police headquarters at 16 Smith Street at about 10 o'clock. He walked all the way to the corner of Eleventh Street and Sixth Avenue, and then became exhausted. At about 11:30 Captain Reynolds, who was walking along Sixth Avenue with Patrolman Delaney, saw a man leaning against a grocer's coal box on the corner. When they reached the spot they discovered the man was Deputy Chief Mackellar.

As soon as Mackellar saw Reynolds, he said, "Oh, I just had a bad spell. It will be over in a minute. I had one before a few days ago, and it passed."

Reynolds and Officer Delaney took Mackellar by the arm and assisted him to his home. John Mackellar died in his home the next morning from heart disease. John Mackellar was known as a courteous, reserved gentleman, whose whole interest in life outside of the police department was centered around his wife and two daughters. On the job, he was known as a fair and competent administrator and leader.

George A. Waddy became a member of the police force of the city of Brooklyn in January 1851 and was appointed sergeant in 1860. He was assigned to the Ninth Sub-Precinct, and when the Ninth became a full-fledged precinct the following year, Waddy was appointed captain. The splendid detective work Waddy performed during the Oterro murder case brought him special attention, and in 1873 he was promoted to inspector and placed in charge of the detectives. When Drill Captain Jewett was reassigned, Waddy assumed his duties, including the responsibility for coordinating department formations at parades and other events, such as the activities at the funerals of Officer Scott and Commissioner Briggs which were only a couple of days apart.. Waddy gave an order that all off duty officers were required to appear for the line of march. When asked about the danger from the current heat wave Inspector Waddy laughed and said, "What are policemen made for if they cannot stand a little fatigue?"

The "little fatigue" caused over a dozen men to fall sick with sunstroke during the two marches. The torture of the march was doubly increased by the uniform the men were ordered to wear consisting of heavy dress coats buttoned to the chin, winter hats, belts, and clubs. With this heavy uniform, by the end of the march most men were as wet as though they had taken baths with their clothes on. While Inspector Waddy characterized the march as slightly fatiguing, he was careful to travel the entire distance of the march himself in a carriage.

Policeman Michael Colohan did not have a carriage to ride in and died two days after marching in the brutal heat. Inspector Waddy was harshly criticized for compelling officers to march a great distance in the broiling sun, and in particular for the death of officer Colohon. He continued in various positions until April 1, 1882, when he was retired on half pay, but he died shortly after his retirement.

CHAPTER 3: WHO WAS GEORGE ZUNDT?

The time period from 1870 to 1898 was Brooklyn's golden age as a city, as it grew from a rural expanse into one of America's largest, most vibrant municipalities. This era was also the golden age of the Brooklyn Police Department as it grew along with the city to become one of the nation's largest, most effective law enforcement agencies, complete with a well-functioning detective division. It was also during this era that George Zundt established himself as the Brooklyn Sleuth.

George Zundt was born in Brooklyn in 1845, in the neighborhood of Court Street and Atlantic Avenue, in what was then the old Tenth Ward. As soon as he turned fourteen, he joined a volunteer fire department, Empire Engine Company No. 19, but his experience as a "fire laddie" was interrupted by the outbreak of the Civil War. Every male member of Zundt's family shouldered a musket in the cause of the Union. Zundt enlisted in Company D, Thirteenth Regiment, in 1861 as a drummer boy, and served for a period of three months. Later, he joined the Fifty-fourth New York Volunteers and served sixteen months in Virginia under Captain Ashely. He participated in every battle in which his corps was engaged. Zundt was severely wounded in the knee at the Battle of Peach Tree Creek, an injury that would plague him for the rest of his life. Zundt left the army in 1864, stayed home with his parents for four or five months before joining the Fifth Connecticut. He left the army for good in 1865.[5]

Zundt's first job after the war was as a cooper, a person trained to make wooden barrels, tubs, and other similar containers. He only kept this job for about six weeks because it didn't pay well enough. He then worked in the carpet business on the corner of Bond and Third Streets for about five years until the business failed. He then drove a truck for a few months until he obtained a contract with the city for lighting lamps. While learning the political ropes in the city to obtain the lighting contract he also learned how to join the police department.

George Zundt was appointed to the Brooklyn Police Department on February 6, 1871, and during his time as a patrolman he served in the First, Eighth-Sub, and Tenth Precincts.

As a uniformed patrolman, Zundt quickly learned the dangers of policework. While assigned to the Tenth Precinct, Zundt was transporting two intoxicated women, named Mary Hayes and Jamie Cummings, to the station house one evening. The problem was that a large segment of the neighborhood did not wish these ladies to be taken into custody. In a well-planned ambush, Zundt was set upon by a gang of rowdies in the vicinity of Nevins and Powers streets. The gang threw stones at Zundt, and finally succeeded in freeing Mary Hayes from the officer, but despite his injuries, Zundt managed to maintain custody of Cummings. Zundt quickly recovered from the attack and Hayes was recaptured several hours later by other officers.[6]

George Zundt and his wife, Mary, experienced a personal tragedy in 1872 when their two-and-a-half-year-old daughter, Ida, died of congestion of the lungs on February 27th. [7]

The harsh realities of patrol can weigh heavily on a police officer, as some of the horrific scenes encountered will be permanently imprinted in their brains. For Patrolman George Zundt, it got no worse than during an early morning patrol near the Gowanus Canal at 9th Street during May of 1872. It was only three months since the death of his daughter when he spied something odd floating in the water. His breathing became more rapid as the object floated closer to him. Without a thought for his uniform, he waded into the canal and snatched the object out of the water. Zundt could hardly breathe as he stood frozen in the waist deep water staring at the blue, lifeless body of a three-week-old infant.[8]

George Zundt witnessed many similar scenes of horror while on patrol. That's why he cherished the peace and quiet that came with his few off duty hours. Sometimes, however, the horror found him even when he was not in uniform.

During June of 1874, Zundt was taking advantage of a rare day off to excavate for a cesspool at the home he had recently moved into on 40th Street between Third and Fourth Avenues, within the confines of the 8th Sub-Precinct. His digging was interrupted by the discovery of a number of human bones consisting of two skulls and other limbs. Among the bones he found a coffin plate with the following inscription: *Catherine Crabb, Age 71, Died March 17, 1839.*

It turned out that Zundt's new home was the site of the old Bergan burying ground, from which bodies were removed six or seven years earlier. Since then, several buildings were constructed on the block. The discovery of the bones, particularly the skulls with hair still attached, caused much excitement in the neighborhood and the Zundt household – excitement George Zundt could have lived without.[9]

During his time as a patrolman, George Zundt was a very active cop, making arrests for all manner of offenses on land, and even on the sea. For example, Zundt arrested two teenage boys while they were in the act of stealing an anchor and chain valued at $190 from the yacht Mary Ann, while the boat was docked at a pier on 35th Street.[10]

Like all cops, Zundt also found himself in the middle of family squabbles. On July 20, 1875, Justice Walsh presided over the case of George N. Carrozi, a well-known musician who was accused of assaulting his father-in-law, Mr. Fredericks, with a cane. Among those who testified in the case was a Mrs. Crittendan, Fredericks daughter and sister to the deceased wife of Carrozi. Justice Walsh ended up dismissing the case and the family appeared content to go on with their lives. Three days later, however, Patrolman Zundt was standing on the corner of Fulton and Boerum Streets at about 7 P.M. He happened to look toward Macomber Square and saw Newton Crittenden, husband of Mrs. Crittenden, strike Carrozi a dozen times with a cane. Carrozi did nothing in return, and was trying to pick up his hat, which had fallen to the ground.

The family found themselves quickly back before Justice Walsh. Newton Crittenden testified that he was passing from his place of business to Hoyt Steet when he met Carrozi, who looked at him in an insolent manner and spat at him. Crittenden turned around and asked him whether he meant to insult him. Carrozi made no reply and Crittenden struck him with the flat of his hand. Carrozi then raised his cane to strike him, but Crittenden took the cane away from him and struck Carrozi a few blows.

George Carrozi testified that as he passed Crittenden on the street he coughed and spit, but not at Crittenden, who stopped and asked Carrozi why he insulted him. Carrozi told Crittenden he did not insult him, but Crittenden proceeded to take his cane away from him and strike him repeatedly with it. Justice Walsh found Crittenden guilty and sentenced him to a fine of $20 or 30-days in jail. Carrozi was acquitted.[11]

CHAPTER 4: DETECTIVE ZUNDT

George Zundt's outstanding record as a patrolman did not go unnoticed, and he was appointed a detective in October 1875 on the recommendation of Police Commissioner Daniel Briggs. Superintendent Patrick Campbell was also strongly in favor of his selection, both on account of Zundt's well known shrewdness, and his knowledge of the German and Polish languages, with which no other member of the squad was acquainted. Zundt went on to establish a record second to none in the department, working on some of the most important criminal cases which had ever occurred in Brooklyn.[12]

"Detectives" were an unknown entity in the 18th century, but Constable De B. Voise conducted the first recorded criminal investigation in Brooklyn. In 1787, a farmer named Bergen, living on Clove Road (roughly where Atlantic Avenue intersects with Classon Avenue) was robbed of his chickens. The theft was performed expertly with the thief leaving no trace or clue of his identity. De B. Voise studied the theft carefully and engaged a partner to go from house to house in the guise of being a feather-buyer. The constable's assistant finally came to the house of a respectable farmer, whose wife offered him a remarkably large number of fresh feathers for sale. Under the pretense of going to get the money to complete the sale, the assistant reported to De B. Voise who promptly returned to the house and arrested the farmer. That criminal, however, was never punished. During the first night of his incarceration in the "calaboose" or "koop," he escaped by simply kicking out the window and walking away.[13]

Detective work in the Brooklyn Police Department came of age after the State Legislature passed the bill on April 5, 1870, making the police department in Brooklyn an independent organization. The new police commissioners, Daniel Briggs and Isaac Van Anden, along with Mayor Martin Kalbfleisch, were responsible for establishing a detective division that would go on to be one of the most important branches in the department.[14]

The detective was one of the most important pieces of police machinery, and the doings of its members generally attracted more attention and interest than those of the ordinary patrol officer, although the latter was frequently called upon to perform duties of equal importance. The vast amount of criminal knowledge locked up in the brain of a detective, and the secrecy which hedged his movements, rendered him, in the estimation of many, one of the most mysterious and important functionaries in society.

The detective division, like the Brooklyn Police Department itself, grew from small beginnings. In January 1851, a regular force of over one hundred men was organized with a chief and four detectives, who were then called chief's aids. In those day the detective quartet were very important functionaries, acting as a bodyguard to the chief or mayor when any special work had to be done. In a short time, a fifth detective was added, and the strength of the squad remained at that level until 1871, when it was reorganized with a sergeant at its head. This reorganization marked an important era in its history. Harry Van Wagner was placed at its head, with the rank of sergeant, and it was managed much the same as if it were a separate precinct. The men no longer went on "flying" expeditions, but were detailed to regular duty, each being selected for that line of business for which he was best fitted, either by experience or expertise.[15]

As the detective division evolved, it began filling with ambitious men – men who were on the lookout for opportunity to display their knowledge and abilities in their chosen line of work. Those who undertook the work without a special liking for it soon resigned. Most of the top detectives believed that a man was born for the profession, not made. He had to be endowed with an extra quantity of good common sense as well as the quality of intellect that could suggest ideas, an excellent memory, particularly for faces, and a good supply of courage and nerve. Then, in addition to these natural qualifications, he must have accumulated experience in the line of human nature and be intimately familiar with the ways and customs of that class of society which disregarded the law.[16]

In 1877 Superintendent Campbell reorganized the Central Office Detective Squad. The squad was composed of ten men, and it was usual for them to be paired in assignments. Campbell distributed them into two classes – the first composed of those whose long experience was considered to give them a better knowledge of detective work than their brethren, who had not been so long in the squad. When George Zundt was appointed a detective, he was assigned to the Central Office and placed in the second class of detectives. [17]

CHAPTER 5: THE ROBBERY OF JOHN CONNORS

The first case with which Detective Zundt had to grapple involved a series of thefts from a well-known Brooklynite named John Connors. Zundt's brilliant management of the case established him as a prominent force in the detective squad.

Two gold watches of considerable value and $1,500 in cash had been stolen from Connors, who resided on Smith Street. There had been no signs of forced entry, so the crime was thought to be the work of a sneak thief who was familiar with the house and Connors' habits. Two or three old hands in the detective squad, after several days' investigation, were forced to acknowledge that they were baffled, and it was hinted that no robbery at all had taken place. Zundt at once suspected that the robbery was the work of a woman who had about a year previous been a domestic in the employment of a relative of Connors, with whom he boarded at the time. Connors, however, had forgotten all about the girl, and told Zundt that he did not think she ever knew where he was living and that she therefore could have nothing to do with the robbery. Zundt, however, thought differently and soon became convinced that he was on the right track by hearing that this same girl was frequently observed in the evening in the neighborhood of Connors' residence. The only description he could obtain of her was that she had red hair and sore eyes and that she usually wore a waterproof cloak, but in a few days, he succeeded in locating her at the residence of her mother in Bushwick. While watching the house one evening Zundt saw her at the door and introduced himself. "How are you, Miss Annie Cody?"

"You are mistaken, sir," was her reply.

"I guess not," responded Zundt. "I believe Mrs. Cody lives upstairs and that you are her daughter. In any event, I will go up and see and will ask you to favor me with your company."

The young woman at first refused, but seeing that the visitor was firm, finally complied and went upstairs with him. Before a word was spoken by either of the women, Zundt, addressing Mrs. Cody said, "Is this your daughter?"

"She is," replied Mrs. Cody, who did not understand the situation. Zundt then explained the object of his visit and informed Mrs. Cody that he would have to take Annie down to police headquarters to answer the charge of grand larceny. Mother and daughter then burst into tears and made a touching appeal to the detective on the ground that Annie's sister was lying at the point of death in the adjoining room, and that it would be cruel to take her away under the circumstances. Zundt at first doubted the truth of the statement, but soon realized it was correct when he found a priest and doctor at the bedside of the patient, who was suffering from a malignant form of fever. There was nothing, however, for Annie to do but accompany Zundt to headquarters and state her case to the Superintendent. Before leaving she requested the detective to allow her to bid her sister goodbye, and to be left alone while doing so. Zundt refused to leave her alone, fearing that she might attempt to make her escape. While leaning over her sister in the bed, Zundt noticed that Annie passed her something she had taken from her pocket, which the sick woman hastily placed under her clothes. In spite of Annie's protests, Zundt insisted on her turning over what she had just slipped to her sister, and it proved to be two pawn tickets for the watches which had been stolen from Connors. Annie then admitted her guilt, and upon being taken before the Superintendent, she made a full confession.

It seemed she had been in the habit of quietly entering Connors' house and secreting herself in a closet in his bedroom, and remaining there until he came home and had fallen asleep. She then came out of her hiding place to ransack his pockets and carry off sums of money which ranged from $10 to $15. All this money she said she spent in furnishing the house in Bushwick, where she lived with her mother and sister. Annie was tried and convicted and sentenced to prison for one year.

CHAPTER 6: THE TOLEDO BLADE

The capture of William Mortimer, known as the "Toledo Blade" was the next important piece of police work accomplished by Zundt. It seemed that Mortimer, accompanied by a middle-aged lady, drove up in grand style to the office of the City Treasurer, in Toldeo Ohio, and leaving his lady companion in the carriage, stepped into the office and coolly walked off with a tin box containing nearly $3,000, which one of the clerks had carelessly left within reach. He managed to make his escape with his plunder, but the woman was arrested. She refused, although offered a pardon, to give the slightest information which might assist the police in effecting the arrest of the fugitive.

Descriptions of the woman and Mortimer were sent out to the various police departments throughout the country, including Brooklyn. On reading the description of the woman, Zundt was struck with its resemblance to that of a Mrs. Childs, who kept a questionable resort at the corner of Fourth Avenue and 27th Street, in Gowanus, and made up his mind to check out the place. The discovery that Mrs. Childs had been absent in the west, as he was informed, for several months, convinced him that he was on the right track, and he immediately opened communication with the chief of police in Toledo, which resulted in establishing the identity of Mrs. Childs as the prisoner there without a doubt. The Toledo Police Department did not have enough evidence to hold Mrs. Childs, so she was released.

Over the next several weeks Detective Zundt kept track of the movement of Mrs. Childs' husband and daughter at their home. His shrewdness was soon brilliantly rewarded, for one pleasant afternoon he observed Mrs. Childs, herself, promenading on Fulton Street with a gentleman who bore a striking resemblance to the individual wanted in Toledo, and whom he did not lose sight of until he found that he was staying at the Clinton House. Later the same evening Zundt paid a visit to Mrs. Childs and playfully remarked, "Lizzie, I'll bet you a bottle of wine you will soon get in trouble. If Mrs. Robbins finds you with her husband again, there will be a row. I tell you, you will lose every hair on your head if you keep walking on Fulton Street with the Washington Market chicken merchant."

"What do you mean?" replied Lizzie, "I don't know any Mr. Robbins, and I never walked on Fulton Street with any man of that name."

"I'll bet you a bottle of wine," replied Zundt, "that I saw you in his company this afternoon."

"Good," said Lizzie. "The wine is mine. The man you saw me with this afternoon was Will Mortimer, a western merchant."

Zundt smiled sweetly, did not prolong the discussion, and with apparent willingness paid for the wine. Mr. Mortimer was snatched that very night, and in his pockets were found $2,000 of the stolen money. The fugitive was accompanied by a young and beautiful lady, whom he had induced to desert her home while he was on his way to Brooklyn, and who was restored in a few days to her parents. The Toledo detectives, who had been all the while groping in the dark, were notified of the arrest and Mortimer was brought there in a few days. He was sentenced to imprisonment for seven years and six months. The Toledo authorities failed to show any substantial appreciation of Zundt's services, although nearly $2,000 was recovered through his work.

CHAPTER 7: THE CRIME OF THE CENTURY

1875 had not been a good year for the Brooklyn community of East New York. A string of robberies and crimes of violence had shrouded the neighborhood in a sense of fear and uneasiness. By December, the community was just beginning to regain its reputation for peace and order.

Martin Segellen had labored on the farm for years. As he walked wearily through the corn stalks, he anticipated just another day working in the field on Deidrich Wessel's East New York farm. On this day, however, something out of the ordinary caught his eye. A woman's shawl lay next to a tall stalk. As he approached the shawl Martin recoiled in horror when he observed a woman's body lying next to the shawl. So, began Brooklyn's crime of the century and the case that made George Zundt the greatest detective no one ever heard of.

At 1:25 P.M. Deidrich Wessel arrived at the East New York station house and reported what had been found in his corn field to Roundsman Herbert. A roundsman was an obsolete rank used in both the Brooklyn and New York police departments during the 19th century. There were no lieutenants during this era, only sergeants, captains, and inspectors. The roundsman was the first line supervisor who assisted the sergeant. The title derived from the fact that this supervisor made "the rounds" to check on the patrol officers. The Roundsman and Officer Brophy proceeded at once to the corn field.

The field in which the body was found was at the foot of Ridgewood Hill, which overlooked it to the north. It was near the reservoir, and almost shaded by the dark and leafless pines that crowned the ridge adjoining the great storage basins. At night, when a traveler passed that way, he was overwhelmed by the solitude.

As the officers traveled across the furrowed land the ground, baked by frost, crackled beneath their feet, and the snow that had fallen like a fine chalk powder, covered all trace of footprints, if any had immediately preceded theirs. The deceased girl lay on her back about four hundred feet from the Jamaica Plank Road and an equal distance from the nearest house. She lay with her knees raised and her face upturned, revealing a sickening wound to her throat. On her right cheek, also was a deep gash over four inches in length, apparently inflicted by a hasty stab, and the palm of her left hand was cut where she possibly seized the murder weapon. Blood marks were upon her clothing and stained the frozen ground. She was bareheaded and wore a light pearl colored underdress and black overskirt, a red and black striped shawl, and a pair of lace shoes. She appeared to be around 20-30 years of age with dark hair and eyes. The earth near the place where she was found bore in several places' indication of a struggle. To Herbert and Brophy, the woman was unknown as neither could recollect ever seeing her before and they had no report of a missing person.

Immediately upon his return to the station house Roundsman Herbert telegraphed to police headquarters, drawing a response at 3 P.M. from Coroner Simms, Captain Crafts, Sergeant Meeks, and Detectives Butts and Van Wagener. They proceeded at once to where the body lay, and a search by the detectives at and around the site succeeded in discovery of the apparent murder weapon when they found a knife hidden in a stack of corn stalks. Coroner Simms took possession of the knife, which was covered with blood. He also took charge of a pair of earrings found upon the deceased. These were common articles of jewelry with pendent drops. In the pocket of her dress was found an unmarked handkerchief, a tailor's thimble, and a three-cent coin. Coroner Simms directed that the body be taken to the East New York station house.

From the time the body was brought to the station house until it was moved to the morgue the next day, there was a steady stream of people passing in and out of the building, all anxious to identify the body. Many of them, mainly women, asserted that they had seen the deceased at some time previous, some indicating that she may have been at a fair in the German Catholic Church a few nights earlier.

Mr. Bennett, proprietor of Bennett's Garden, recognized a resemblance between the dead girl and a young woman who came to his place a few days earlier inquiring about the whereabouts of her brother. Another man thought he had seen the girl employed as a servant in the household of Mr. Rapaljes, of New Lots, but that claim proved incorrect.

When the body was removed to the morgue her identity was still a mystery. The first solid clue was provided by Mr. Augustus Taylor, a young man who positively identified the body of the murdered woman as that of a female who rode to East New York in the same car with him on Sunday afternoon. He said she was accompanied by a young man of slight build and a heavy dark mustache. Taylor said the male and female got off the car together at East New York.

At noon on Wednesday, three men entered the coroner's office and asked to see one of the coroners. The only person in the office was a reporter from the Daily Eagle, who determined that one of the men, named Pisach Alexander, thought the deceased girl may be his sister, 19-year-old Sarah Alexander. In his conversation with the man, the reporter learned that Sarah Alexander was a Jewish girl who had lived in Manhattan after coming to America from a part of Poland that was then part of Russia about a year and a half earlier. She lived for about ten months with her cousins, the Rubenstein's, who ran a dry goods store at 83 Bayard Street, in Manhattan, before moving in with her brother. Pisach said Sarah worked as a tailoress, but of late had been out of work.[18]

Pisach said that on Sunday at about 1 P.M. Sarah left his house to go to her cousin's Bayard Street home. She stayed there with Mr. and Mrs. Rubenstein and their son Pasach Rubenstein until about 4 P.M. Once she departed the Rubenstein's home she was never seen again.

When no coroner returned to the office, the reporter accompanied Pisach and his companions to the morgue. When they arrived at the morgue, they found that the body had not arrived yet. While they waited the reporter continued to talk to Pisach. He said his sister was a very religious girl who never went around with men. While still waiting for the body to arrive Israel Rubenstein, an older man and the owner of the dry goods store, appeared at the morgue and engaged the reporter in conversation, including a rather remarkable story. Mr. Rubenstein said that on Sunday afternoon he saw Sarah in his store, and that when she departed about 4 P.M. she was all alone. He said that the next information he received was that Sarah was missing. Then, unprompted, the old man continued to tell the reporter about a conversation he had with his son Pasach on Monday morning after Sarah's brother had come looking for herh.

Pasach said to his father, "Father, I had a terrible dream last night about Sarah."

"What was it?"

"Oh, father," he said, "I dreamed that I saw Sarah and that she was killed and was ten miles out of New York City, and I thought in my dream that she wanted me to bury her."

Pasach Rubenstein was the oldest of three sons, all of whom were married. Pasach's wife, however, was in Russia, and it was apparent to all who knew them that Pasach was fond of Sarah. Sarah was a frequent visitor to the store on Bayard Street, even after she moved in with her brother, and she spent most of her time at Bayard Street in the company of Pasach Rubenstein. About a year earlier, when Sarah was still living with the Rubenstein's, Pasach became very ill with a serious disease, and Sarah insisted on being his nurse. She attended to Pasach day and night, and when he recovered, Pasach began paying a great deal of attention to Sarah. Because they had spent so much time together while he was sick, no one really took notice of the intimacy developing between Pasach and Sarah after he recovered.

As far as Israel Rubenstein was concerned, Sarah left his home alone at around 4 P.M. on Sunday, and his son Pasach departed alone about 5 P.M. Pasach did not tell his father where he was going and when he returned home at 10 P.M. he didn't tell him where he had been.

The newspapers had given such a detailed description of the murder victim, it prompted her brother and two friends to believe the victim was Sarah. Even Israel Rubenstein travelled to Brooklyn to check the body. Conspicuously missing from the Brooklyn Morgue was the man who supposedly cared the most for Sarah Alexander – Pasach Rubenstein.

When the body finally arrived at the morgue, Pisach Alexander identified his sister as the murder victim. For Inspector Waddy, the head of Brooklyn's detectives at the time, a few pieces of this murder puzzle had fallen into place. The Inspector had learned that Pasach Rubenstein's wife was on her way from Russia to the United States. Waddy had also been told that Sarah spoke no English, so it was likely she was with someone who spoke Polish, the language Sarah spoke.

While everyone was still at the morgue, Captain Crafts was able to produce six men who had ridden the 6:08 Broadway car from the South 7th Street Ferry. Inspector Waddy took the men into a private room where they all identified Sarah Alexander and stated a male companion with dark features who wore a slouched hat had been in the car with her.

Captain Crafts had delayed Israel Rubenstein from leaving the morgue, and now Inspector Waddy had a plan to get a description of Pasach Rubenstein.

"Say, Rubenstein," Waddy called out, "I think one of your sons was here a minute ago. He wanted to see you, but think he left again."

"So?" the old man shrugged, "where did he go?"

"I don't know," Waddy replied. "Perhaps he'll come back." The Inspector shook his head. "I'm not sure that it was your son, but I think it was. He had black whiskers and beard and a mustache."

"Yes," Israel nodded, "my son Pasach has black hair."

"What does he look like?" Waddy asked.

"Oh, he is tall – bigger than me – and thin."

"What sort of hat does he wear?"

Rubenstein pointed to a man in the corner wearing a slouched hat. "Like that, but with a bigger brim."

There was still much to discover in this murder mystery, but Inspector Waddy knew what the next step had to be. Pasach Rubenstein had to be taken into custody. It was time for George Zundt to enter the game.

Inspector Waddy directed Detectives Corwin and Zundt to travel to Manhattan to pick up Pasach Rubenstein. When the detectives arrived at 83 Bayard Street, Pasach was not there. Mrs. Rubenstein was working alone in the store, which appeared to be a dry goods and jewelry store combined. Mrs. Rubenstein said her son Pasach had gone out, but that she expected him to return before long. Detective Corwin hurried back to Brooklyn in case Pasach had decided to join his father at the morgue. In the meantime, Detective Zundt remained in the store and engaged Mrs. Rubenstein in a search for a pair of gloves. Zundt tried to appear very anxious to purchase the gloves, but no matter how hard she tried, Mrs. Rubenstein could not come up with gloves to suit him. She turned over her whole stock, but the detective still could not find exactly what he wanted. Finally, when there were no more gloves to look at, Pasach Rubenstein entered the store. He ran in as if he was being pursued by someone. As he ran toward the back of the store, Zundt called out, "Mr. Rubenstein, I want you to come over to the morgue in Brooklyn. They have your cousin there and the coroner wants you to identify the body before he can give it up."

"My brothers and father are there," said Pasach, "they can identify it."

Zundt shook his head. "The coroner wants you – he wants one more of her relatives to identify her before he gives the body up for burial."

"Oh, no, no," said Pasach, putting up his hands, "I don't want to go – I don't want to go." Then he ran into the back room and brought out a pair of earrings. "See," he said, "I gave that girl a pair like this."

"Yes, she has a pair like that," Zundt agreed, "but I still need you to come over to Brooklyn with me."

"Oh, no, no, no," wailed Pasach, "I don't want to go over there."

"Oh, come on," said the annoyed detective, "come along now or I'll take you by force – that's all. You've got to come, do you hear?" As he said that Zundt caught hold of Pasach by the collar. Pasach turned pale with fright and appeared to be at the point of vomiting. Zundt pushed him out of the store and started him on the trip to Brooklyn.

When Zundt brought Pasach into the morgue a reporter asked if Rubenstein had said anything during the trip. "Not a word," Zundt said. "He never spoke to me nor I to him all the way over. He never even asked what he was arrested for."

While Detective Zundt was bringing Pasach Rubenstein across the river, Dr. Shepard arrived at the morgue to perform the post-mortem examination on Sarah Alexander. Dr. Shepard was joined by Coroner Simms, Inspector Waddy, and Drs. Nesbitt and Brady in the dissection room of the morgue. The body had been placed on a marble slab as Dr. Shepard began the examination by washing off the blood from the face and arms and cleaning the dirt from her knees. The wounds to the neck and face were also washed after which Dr. Shepard recorded a description of the lacerations. Dr. Shepard next made the usual incision in the body and made the stunning discovery that Sarah Alexander had been approximately five months pregnant.

By the time Detective Zundt arrived, the morgue was filled with Pasach Rubenstein's relatives and supporters. They were all upset that a religious man such as Pasach should be accused of such a brutal crime. Zundt kept Pasach in a separate room while Detective Dave Corwin kept the throng of supporters from reaching Pasach. Corwin finally had to take Pasach's uncle, Moses Harris, by the scruff of the neck and forcibly eject him from the morgue.

When the post-mortem examination was completed, Coroner Simms called for Zundt to bring Pasach into the dissection room. As soon as Pasach saw the dead form under the shawl he shrank back and let out a moan of terror.

"Do you know that girl?" Coroner Simms asked.

"Yes," said Pasach. He was standing away from the table with his body pressed up against the wall. He seemed to want to get as far away from the body as possible.

"Step around here," directed the coroner. "You can't see the face from where you are."

Pasach wouldn't move, so Detective Zundt pushed him over until he could see the face.

"Have you seen this girl before," Coroner Simms asked.

"Yes, I seen her. Yes, yes, I seen her." Pasach's face was more deathly looking than the girl on the slab, and he kept shuffling backwards to get away from the body.

Zundt pushed Pasach back toward the body. Coroner Simms repeated his prior inquiries, "Are you sure you know this girl?" As he asked the question Simms removed the shawl from the girl's neck revealing the horrific wounds.

Pasach shrieked in terror as he pulled out of the grasp of the coroner and Detective Zundt and jumped backwards, holding up his hands to shield his eyes from the horrible sight.

Detective Zundt transported Pasach to police headquarters where he would be formally interrogated. Pasach did not speak English well, and since Zundt was fluent in both Polish and German, he conducted the questioning of Pasach Rubenstein. Zundt did not find the interrogation to be easy. Whenever he asked a question Pasach would wander away from it and commence to tell a long story, chiefly to the effect that he was an honest man. Zundt was losing his patience, but finally Pasach began answering to his activities on Sunday. Pasach said he got up at 6 A.M. and went to the synagogue. He said he stayed there until 8 A.M., and then returned home and ate breakfast. Pasach said at 9 A.M. he travelled to Maiden Lane to see a man on business, but the man didn't show up for the appointment. Pasach would not reveal the name of the man he was supposed to meet. He continued that he returned home and had supper at about 12:30 P.M., after which his went to 193 Canal Street to see John Moloskie and then returned home again. Pasach said he wasn't sure of the time, but he then traveled to 342 32nd Street to collect a commission for a chain he had sold for William Jacobs. Pasach said he then returned home. He was not sure the time he got home, but he remembered it was not dark yet.

"Was Sarah Alexander there when you got home?" Zundt asked.

"Yes," Pasach replied, "she waited on me at dinner and poured me a cup of tea."

"Well, what did you do then?" the detective asked.

"I went to the synagogue."

"Where was Sarah?"

"She was at my house. I left her there when I went to the synagogue."

"Well, what next?" Zundt continued.

"I came home from the synagogue. I don't know what time it was, and then went to 115 Division Street and 138 Division Street."

"Who did you see there?" Zundt asked.

"No one," Pasach responded. "I have friends there, but no one was home."

"What did you do then?"

"I went home"

"What time did you arrive home?"

"It was eight o'clock."

"What did you do then?"

"I went to bed."

That was all Pasach would say. When Zundt tried to open new lines of questions Pasach would claim he did not understand the detective.

Zundt finally shook his head in disgust and turned to Superintendent Campbell. "Damn him, he won't talk anymore at all."

Pasach Rubenstein was lodged in a cell in the First Precinct while Detective Zundt returned to Manhattan seeking more information. His first stop was a return to 83 Bayard Street to speak with Pasach's mother. The building was a six-story tenement house with the dry goods store on the first floor and Mrs. Rubenstein's apartment in the back. Inside that rear apartment is where Detective Zundt found Mrs. Rubenstein and a dozen other women and children crammed inside a small room. Mrs. Rubenstein was a portly woman who wore a full length sacque and a wig. Detective Zundt did not wish to reveal his foreign language fluency, so he questioned Mrs. Rubenstein in English. After several minutes of questioning Zundt began to wonder if he was questioning the correct person. This woman seemed to know very little about Pasach Rubenstein, particularly his activities on the prior Sunday. George Zundt paused and took a deep breath. He should have expected this reaction from Mrs. Rubenstein. The newspapers in Manhattan were filled with stories about her son being the prime suspect in the murder of Sarah Alexander, so her tight lipped response was natural. Zundt did no better when he changed the subject to Sarah Alexander. All Mrs. Rubenstein would say was that her son was an honest, religious man who spent all his time at the synagogue and working in their store. Mrs. Rubenstein was not going to stand for anyone else providing information to the detective. When a woman in the room began to talk about seeing Sarah on Sunday, Mrs. Rubenstein quickly cut her off and told her to shut her mouth in German, a warning easily understood by Zundt. He realized trying to garner information from Mrs. Rubenstein or any of her friends or relatives would be a dead end.

The next morning all the men who had identified Sarah Alexander as being present on the car they were riding in on Sunday were brought to the First Precinct. All of them positively identified Pasach Rubenstein as being with Sarah in the car.

The evidence against Pasach Rubenstein was beginning to build up. There were the inconsistencies in Pasach's story, including his claim that he had not been to Brooklyn, even though six witnesses placed him in the car with Sarah. A motive had also been developed. The investigation had revealed indications of an intimate relationship between Pasach and Sarah. If this were true, the relationship would not have been able to be kept secret for much longer, considering that Sarah was five months pregnant when she was killed. Add to this the fact that Pasach's wife was on her way from Russia to New York City, and Pasach would have had a strong motive to eliminate Sarah before his wife arrived.

The evidence was building, but it was all circumstantial. George Zundt realized strong physical evidence would be required to convict Pasach for the murder, and he was determined to find it.

There had been several sets of footprints at the crime scene that, due to the nature of the cold weather, were likely still intact. Pasach's clothing, including his boots, had been retained as evidence. George Zundt set off for the corn field in possession of Pasach's boots as well as the shoes Sarah Alexander had been wearing. When he arrived at the scene of the crime, his suspicions were correct. Pasach's boots were a perfect fit for the larger footprints in the area and Sarah's shoes fit perfectly in the smaller prints. Additionally, the dirt in the cornfield was lighter and of a different texture than other dirt in the city. Coroner Simms identified the dirt embedded in Pasach's boots as being the type found in the corn field. Also embedded in Pasach's boot was a piece of corn stalk.

The noose was beginning to tighten around Pasach Rubenstein, but George Zundt still wanted to fit one more important piece into the puzzle – the murder weapon. Finding the origin of the knife would be like finding a needle in a haystack, but at least Detective Zundt may be able to work with a smaller haystack. There was a unique aspect to the knife in that it appeared to be flawed and not in condition for sale. It was a long shot, but George Zundt set off for Manhattan again in search of someone who could identify the knife. Zundt began his search early Thursday morning and by two o'clock he had visited over one hundred knife dealers, without success. Detective Zundt was just about worn out when he entered the shop of a man named Eckhoff, on Essex Street. Zundt repeated the ritual of displaying the knife, and after giving it a casual glance, Mr. Eckhoff said the knife was a peculiar make, and that Gustave Simon, whose store was at 138 Division Street, was the only manufacturer of that type of knife. The revelation reinvigorated Detective Zundt and he hurried to Simon's small store, where he found Gustave Simon and his 13-year-old daughter, Augusta. Zundt got right to the point. Standing by the door he held up the weapon and asked Mr. Simon if he made such a knife. The dealer gave it only a casual glance, shrugged and said that he did make the knife. Zundt moved up to the counter and handed the knife to Simon and asked him if he ever remembered seeing this knife before. Without hesitation, Simon said that the knife belonged to him and must have been stolen, as it was condemned and not suitable for sale. Simon pointed to the three rivets which he said were unique features in his knives. He also pointed to the rough state of the handle, which he said made the knife unsuitable for sale.

Detective Zundt was facing another dead end, but he asked Simon to accompany him to Brooklyn to meet with Superintendent Campbell. Simon again identified the knife but could not account for the manner in which it had left his store. Later that evening when Simon had returned to his home, he told his daughter about his experience in Brooklyn. Augusta had been present in the store when Detective Zundt arrived, but she quickly departed and did not hear any of his questions. When she heard her father's story, Augusta revealed that she had sold the condemned knife to a man sometime on Monday of the prior week. When Mr. Simon communicated the new information to Brooklyn police headquarters, Detective Zundt whisked Augusta Simon to Brooklyn.

Once she was comfortably settled in police headquarters, Augusta said that at about four o'clock in the afternoon during Monday of the previous week a man entered the store and asked to see some cigar knives. Augusta said she showed the man many knives, but he tossed all of them aside. She said the man was about to leave the store when he noticed the rough, unfinished, condemned knife lying on the other side of the counter. Augusta said the man asked to see the knife and he toyed with it in his hand for several minutes as if deciding whether to buy it or not. She said she warned the man that it was a rejected knife, but the man said it would serve his purpose, and they closed the deal for twenty cents.

Pasach Rubenstein had been moved from the First Precinct to the Raymond Street Jail. Detective Zundt escorted Augusta to the jail where Rubenstein was brought out to the front office. As soon as he entered the office, Augusta began to cry with fright. She turned to Detective Zundt and said, "That is the man who purchased the knife."

Pasach Rubenstein said nothing as he stared at the floor. [19]

Every effort was made by the friends of Rubenstein to influence the action of the detective. Shortly before the trial Zundt was approached in the interest of Rubenstein and he was informed that $7,000 would be at his disposal if he would allow Augusta Simon, from whom Rubenstein purchased the knife, to be taken from his house, where she had been placed for safekeeping, but the big bribe was not sufficient to tempt the faithful detective, and a closer watch was kept over the important witness.[20]

Rubenstein's family and supporters failed in their endeavors and when they saw how steadfastly Zundt adhered to his duty they became greatly enraged. Subsequently, they never missed an opportunity of manifesting their hatred. Their animosity appeared to increase day by day and after his testimony at the trial they made open and deadly threats against him. Rubenstein's father and older brother, Jacob, were especially bitter toward Zundt. Whenever they were in his presence they spat toward him, shook their clenched fists at him and scowled with great ferocity. After Detective Zundt testified at the trial, Pasach's father and daughter spoke in severe terms of how damaging his testimony was, and they both said that one day Zundt would be sorry for what he had done.[21]

When the jury pronounced him guilty, Pasach Rubenstein raised his hands, threw his head back, fixed his eyes on the judge and cried in a piercing tone, "I don't want to give up my blood."

The scene inside the courtroom was chaotic. Those in the gallery mounted seats and strained to see everything going on. Judge Moore brought the room to order and went forward with the sentencing. "Rubenstein, it is now the duty of the Court to pronounce on you its sentence for the crime of which you have been convicted. Your case has been patiently and carefully tried by a jury of peculiar intelligence. Your counsel has defended you with an ability and zeal which could not be surpassed, but they have labored in vain for you. The terrible, might I say providential, circumstances have been too overwhelming. I will not recapitulate the history of your crime. It is too horrible to contemplate. One, who had a right by ties of race, religion, and blood, to look to you for protection, was by an atrocious act enticed to a lonely spot and butchered without mercy. The law not only requires that you should be fairly tried, but it gives you time to prepare for death, which you brutally denied to your victim, Listen to the sentence of the Court which is: That you be taken to the jail from which you came, and on Friday, the 24th of March, between the hours of nine in the morning and two in the afternoon, you be hanged by the neck until you are dead, and may God have mercy on your soul."

At the conclusion of the sentencing, Rubenstein blurted, "I am not satisfied!"

Rubenstein was placed in one of the "condemned cells" in the Raymond Street Jail. Those cells were reserved for prisoners awaiting execution. While incarcerated, Rubenstein asked to see Detective Zundt and Pisach Alexander, the brother of the murdered girl. When the visitors were in the cell Rubenstein turned to Alexander and declared his innocence. He then turned toward Zundt and commenced making accusations and threats. "You have brought me to the gallows. I am a doomed man, and you are the sole cause of placing me in the position I am in now. My blood will be on you and will follow your wife and your children. You will suffer for this, it may not be this month or next month, but my blood shall follow you, and my kindred will not forget the thing you have done."

Detective Zundt said he was only doing his duty, but Rubenstein continued to shake with anger, "You have frightened my witnesses from coming over here to swear in my behalf, and you have threatened that they would be harmed if they dared to speak the truth of me."

Zundt again tried to explain that he was doing his duty, but Rubenstein would not hear of it, again repeating that the detective and his family would suffer, and that his blood would follow them until a terrible revenge had been obtained. Rubenstein went on to say that he wanted to make this declaration in front of the victim's brother and to declare his innocence.

Pasach Rubenstein never made it to the gallows. He died in his jail cell on May 4th, 1876, from causes directly brought about by lack of proper nourishment and the unhygienic environment of the cell. Some say Rubenstein, in effect, committed suicide. It was not certain that he deliberately adopted a course that would lead to his death, but he constantly refused to eat much of his food and had refused to wash himself. Added to this he observed long and rigid periods of fasting, which combined with his filthy surroundings, served to completely undermine his health.[22]

On the day of Rubenstein's funeral, a dramatic scene occurred in the morgue which clearly indicated the hatred and desire for vengeance that the relatives of the murderer felt. Rubenstein's remains had been laid out in a small room at the rear of the morgue. The corpse reposed in a plain, rough wooden box. It was partially covered with a course blanket, but the face was visible and the eyes stared in the stony horror of death. Although it was broad daylight, a candle flickered at either end of the coffin, and at the side, half kneeling on the floor and half clinging to the wooden box, the father of Rubenstein, frantic with grief, moaned painfully. Detective Zundt, accompanied by another detective, suddenly entered the room. His appearance had an electrical effect on the aged and weeping father. He threw himself on his son's body, as if to protect it from desecration, and then, drawing himself up, with blazing eyes and quivering lips he pointed a menacing finger toward Zundt. "Curses on you; the curse of the God of my fathers on you," he exclaimed in broken English. Then he struck himself on his chest and glaring at Zundt mumbled something about his broken heart.

The detective appeared to take the matter very coolly. He regarded the enraged father with a cynical glance, and taking his cigar from his mouth, he observed, "Too bad, old man, but if you don't want me to look at him, I won't." Zundt then turned on his heel and walked away, while Rubenstein in subdued tones continued to invoke curses upon him.[23]

At the funeral the bitterness of the Rubenstein family found full expression. When the hearse and the carriages reached the old Washington Cemetery, which nestled away down in one corner of the town of Gravesend, the father and his brother Jacob gave full vent to their passions and talked in the most violent and threatening tone.

"Oh, God," cried Jacob Rubenstein, as the coffin was lowered into the ground, "rain down your curses on Zundt and on all his family. Give us the opportunity to wreak vengeance on him. He killed Pasach. His hands are red with his blood. May the rats eat him, and the dogs tear him to pieces."

Rubenstein's father prayed for vengeance and said that the curse of heaven would light on Zundt and the District Attorney both of whom, he said, had been seeking his poor boy's blood. Rubenstein's sister was also greatly agitated and joined in the denunciation of Zundt and the District Attorney.

Zundt brushed of the hostile language as empty threats made by people suffering profound grief. Several weeks later, however, Pisach Alexander, the brother of Sarah Alexander, traveled to Brooklyn to see Detective Zundt. He informed Zundt that he had received information that a deep and villainous plot against him and his family was underway, and it involved nothing less than the abduction of one of Zundt's children. Zundt was startled at first by this revelation. At the time Zundt had five children, all boys, who were attending Public School No. 32 at the corner of Hoyt and President Streets. Zundt took no special precautions for the safety of his children, commenting, "The cowards wouldn't dare to steal one of them or try to injure them in any way. They know better than to interfere with me or my family." Zundt was correct in that no attempt was ever made to abduct one of his children. But what about the curse?[24]

Those of a superstitious nature paused to consider the Rubenstein curse in 1880 when Zundt's youngest son was suddenly stricken with an illness and died.[25] In 1883 the curse seemed to take full hold of the Zundt family when within the space of a few weeks, five year old Walter Zundt was seriously injured when he caught his foot in the railroad track at Ninth Street, another son was accidentally shot in the hand, and the detective's sister died.[26]

A few years later, in 1887, Zundt almost lost another son through a strange accident. Charles A. Zundt, came near losing his life as a result of the family dog. During Detective Zundt's absence from home, the family was under the watchful eye of the dog, who was prompt to discover strangers and treat them all as he might be expected to treat desperate criminals. In order that he may not swoop down upon too many suspected malefactors, the dog was kept chained in the yard during the daytime.

Young Mr. Zundt ate breakfast late in the morning and then prepared to shave himself. The dog was securely fastened just outside the window where the young man was shaving, and just as young Zundt raised his head and had his razor at his throat, the dog let out a tremendous bark that startled Zundt, causing him to turn quickly. Unfortunately, his head moved in the opposite direction then the hand holding the razor, the result being a serious gash to his throat. A call was immediately sent to the Long Island College Hospital and Ambulance Surgeon Shepard responded and sewed up the wound. A policeman, who had been informed that the case was an attempted suicide, decided upon further investigation, that the only culprit was the dog.[27]

In 1892 another tragedy struck the Zundt's when Detective Zundt's grandson, six-year-old George E. Zundt, died after a sudden illness.[28]

Was it the Rubenstein curse, or just a string of bad luck? One thing that was as real in the 19th century as it is today is the dark sense of humor possessed by police officers. Medical and psychological professionals have studied this phenomenon for years, and have concluded that this dark sense of humor, which many may consider inappropriate, is a defense mechanism to deal with the horrific scenes a cop deals with on patrol. A very hardcore example of the "dark" police humor occurred less than two months after Pasach Rubenstein died, and Detective Zundt had received the wrath of the Rubenstein family curse.

A newspaper article detailed fourth annual excursion of the Atlantic Chowder Club that was held on the Long Island Sound at Great Neck, Long Island. The article said there were about were about three hundred people present on the steamer William Tittamer, and that many of the attendees were police officers. The article listed some of the attendees, including, George Zundt, alias "Rubenstein" [29]

CHAPTER 8: YOU CAN'T TELL A BOOK BY ITS COVER

Several weeks earlier a woman named Margaret Creemer and her daughter, Elizabeth Creemer were arrested by Detective Zundt on a charge of having stolen two pieces of silk from a dry goods store on Fulton Street. One of the pieces was stolen on a Wednesday, and the other on the Saturday following, and it was then that Mrs. Creemer and her daughter were arrested.

When taken to police headquarters, the mother, apparently a very respectable woman, denied the thefts but when searched, the silk was found on her person, at which point she confessed and burst into tears. She said that want drove her to steal, and alleged that her husband was away in Canada looking for work, and her sons were out of employment, and that one of her son's was sick and in need of a physician's care, who was now suing her for the unpaid bill.

The dry goods store owner, Mr. Thorburn was sympathetic to Mrs. Creemer's plight and told the district attorney he would not press charges unless he was compelled to do so.

Mrs. Creemer swore that her daughter had nothing to do with the theft, prompting Justice Walsh to dismiss the case against her daughter and to set very low bail on Mrs. Creemer, which was promptly paid by a friend.

On the day that Mrs. Creemer failed to appear in court, an anonymous letter was received at police headquarters. The letter was written in German and was read by Detective Zundt. Zundt smiled as he read that Mrs. Creemer's story of poverty was all a lie, and that she was actually a successful professional shoplifter who had returned to Canada to ply her trade. [30]

After his experience with Mrs. Creemer, it was understandable when Detective Zundt rolled his eyes in Justice Walsh's courtroom several days later when Mary Gould passionately proclaimed her innocence. Zundt had arrested the good-looking young woman for stealing a lace shawl from an elderly gentleman named H.G. Webb, who resided on Franklin Avenue.

Mr. Webb entered the courtroom shortly after Zundt and his prisoner and stated that six months earlier he had taken Mrs. Gould into his home where she resided until a week ago. When she left the home, Mr. Webb said that Gould stole a lace shawl worth $75 and that she was still in possession of diamonds he had loaned her that were worth $500. As Webb was finishing his statement Detective Zundt was surprised to see someone else enter the courtroom and take a seat behind Mary Gould. Ex-Detective Lovett had been a detective assigned to the Central Office for only six weeks when he was dismissed from the department for drunkenness.

It didn't take a detective to figure out that there was some relationship between Gould and Lovett, for when Webb had finished making his accusation, Mary Gould cried out that Webb had given the shawl to her, prompting Lovett to stand up, tap her on the shoulder and say, "Didn't you tell me you would give it back to him."

Justice Walsh quickly admonished Lovett to sit down and say nothing to the defendant. Lovett refused to sit, and two officers assigned to the courtroom had to physically remove the struggling Lovett from the room.

Once Lovett was dragged from the room, Mary Gould said, "I am glad you put him out because he has been the cause of this trouble between me and Mr. Webb."

Justice Walsh asked for an explanation, and Mary stated that when she was divorced from her husband, Webb had given her both the shawl and the diamonds and that he frequently put his arms around her neck and said she should be his wife. Mary said she lived in Webb's home in the capacity of a companion until about a week ago. Mary said she had maintained a casual friendship with Lovett, and that Webb had become jealous of that friendship, which motivated him to accuse her of the theft.

Hearing Mary's words seemed to soften Webb, who then expressed regret at having had her arrested, and when Justice Walsh decided to adjourn the case to a later date, Webb wanted to post her $1,000 bond. The judge explained that the person bringing the charges could not post the bond, so Webb contacted a friend to post the bail. All Detective Zundt could do is sigh and smile at a somewhat happy ending.[31]

CHAPTER 9: THE CAPTAIN GOES DOWN WITH THE SHIP

Captain William Hammond, who years ago really did go on board a ship and had since assumed the title of captain, was arrested in the Fourth Precinct on a charge of obtaining about $1,000 worth of goods under false pretenses. The captain was sixty years of age and was an old timer in the confidence business. He had done almost everything to make money and had generally been successful, and had also managed on many occasions to avoid well deserved punishment.

He was "in" with the first-class New York thieves and was known to every detective of any account as a "crooked man" and a first class one, too. He had manipulated forged and stolen bonds and done it so adroitly that other people had been arrested for the offense, he himself cleverly escaping arrest. And yet, the captain would not be taken for a swindler. He was old now and gray headed and very bulky. He had a pleasing countenance and a peculiarly mild demeanor.

His latest exploit for which he was arrested was swindling a number of New York storekeepers. He first rented a stylish house on the corner of Fifth Avenue and 85th Street and paid a month's rent in cash. He then paid a visit to E.W. Baxter's furniture store on Canal Street and informed the store owner that he was about to start a first-class boarding house on Fifth Avenue, and desired Mr. Baxter to accompany him to the house, see each room and take note of what furniture would be needed.

Mr. Baxter went with the captain, and both went through the house, and Mr. Baxter suggested a carpet of different descriptions for each room they visited. Mr. Baxter surveyed the parlor and suggested that a fine satin covered lounge should be placed there, along with several other pieces of expensive furniture. Baxter asked the captain what he thought. The captain was charmed with Mr. Baxter's taste and informed him that he did not wish to spare any expense, and so ordered Mr. Baxter to send the furniture immediately.

The furniture man willingly took the order and as he did so, the captain playfully remarked, "Now, I want this furniture to be just as you represent it. I am an old sea dog you know, and don't know very much about these matters, so I shall have to rely on you not to cheat me."

Mr. Baxter promised him that when he sent the furniture to the house, he would be pleased with it. "Well," said the captain, "deliver your furniture and then send your bill up and I'll pay it."

So, Mr. Baxter left the Fifth Avenue mansion, returned to his store and filled up the order, sending to the house about $1,000 worth of fine furniture. The captain in the meantime called upon Mr. Dumbsday, of East 9th Street, and ordered a $500 piano to be sent to the house immediately. As with Mr. Baxter, the captain told Dumbsday to send him the bill. Mr. Dumdsday believed he had a good customer and did not hesitate to send the piano to the house on Fifth Avenue. The piano and all the furniture arrived before nightfall, at which time the captain hired three furniture wagons and had the new furniture and the piano taken to an auction room, and there he sold them at considerably less than their value.

Mr. Baxter and Mr. Dumdsday called at the mansion with their respective bills on the same day, and found to their utter astonishment, that their property was not there. That was not all. When the house was searched it was found that the captain had removed the range and sold it. He had taken out the mantelpieces and disposed of them. He unscrewed the chandeliers and converted them into cash. He even slipped off the bronze doorknobs and faucets and sold them. It was a wonder that he didn't attempt to sell the whole house. The next thing to do was to find the old sea dog, and that proved to be a hard matter.

This little transaction occurred a little over a year earlier, and since then, New York detectives had been hunting high and low for Captain William Hammond. At last, they came to the Brooklyn Central Office and asked for assistance in finding their man. They wanted to know if

Brooklyn had a man who knew the captain, whereupon George Zundt spoke up and said he knew him.

When asked if he could find him, Zundt said he thought he could. After some brief groundwork, Zundt discovered that Captain Hammond had a sister living on Walworth Street, and he suggested to the New York detectives that they should accompany him to begin watching the house. The surveillance began early in the morning, with Zundt watching the rear of the house because he believed that if the captain was to come or go from the house he would use the back door.

At about 4:30 P.M. on the first day of the surveillance Zundt observed the captain's burly form at the back door. He was in his shirt sleeves and smoking leisurely. Zundt motioned to the New York detectives. "There's your man," he said, and all three went to the house and arrested him.

"What's this for?" said the trembling captain.

"I guess you know best," replied Zundt, who quietly slipped handcuffs on his wrists.

The captain looked like a very crestfallen sea dog when he was brought to police headquarters, but he said very little. He was brought before Superintendent Campbell and then locked up in the First Precinct station house. The captain would not be going to sea again fr quite some time. [32]

CHAPTER 10: A NIGHT AT THE FIGHTS

In today's NYPD, a reality of the job that most detectives could live without is having to work a uniformed detail. It is common for detectives to be ordered into uniform to work at a parade, sporting event, demonstration, and an assortment of other crowd gathering events. Most detectives would rather not don the uniform, unless, of course, they are being paid overtime. Although they were not required to wear a uniform, 19th century Brooklyn detectives like George Zundt were also required to work at certain large events alongside their uniformed brethren.

During the 19th century boxing was one of the most popular sporting events in Brooklyn, but ironically, it was practically illegal in the State of New York. Brooklynites, especially those who gravitated to the seedier sections of Coney Island, tended not to let little things like the law get in the way of a good time. The New York State Legislature had passed "An act to prevent Prize Fighting" in 1859. The act of boxing was not illegal per se but fighting for prize money was deemed to be an affront to public decency. And so it came to pass that on a mild June evening in 1876 the city of Brooklyn sanctioned a bout the public had been screaming for, and Detective George Zundt learned there was more to being a detective than just investigating crimes. [33]

The many gas jets in the Brooklyn Rink shone upon the large gathering of sporting men on that evening, the occasion being the bout between Billy Edwards, the lightweight champion, and Steve Taylor, the Jersey City heavyweight, for $1,000. A large majority of the representatives of "the fancy" present were New York men, sprinkled in with a number of Brooklynites and a few enthusiastic individuals from New Jersey. The vast auditorium was brilliantly illuminated and lavishly decorated with small American flags, but even the glaring light and profusion of color failed to relieve to any appreciable extent the cheerless and dreary aspect of the immense interior, which forced upon the mind of the observer that he was in a large, clumsy, overgrown barn.

At the head of the rink, near the stage, which in the days of summer concerts served as a music stand, a ring was pitched. It was 24-feet in diameter and consisted of a thick rope supported by posts. The ring was surrounded by chairs, which were filled as soon as the doors were opened. There were about 2,000 people present and the police were under the command of Sergeant Rogers. Besides the uniformed presence, the detective squad, including George Zundt, were also assigned to the event, together with Superintendent Campbell and Inspector Waddy. The time fixed for the beginning of the match was 8 P.M., and at that hour the large audience became very uneasy, manifesting their impatience by stamping, whistling and clapping their hands. Shortly after, Harry Hill, the referee and master of ceremonies entered the ring to a warm outburst of applause as the spectators immediately settled back in their seats.

The first hour was occupied by a wrestling match and some rather indifferent sparring by amateurs. At 9:30 a murmur among the spectators, followed by uproarious applause, announced the arrival of the "big guns" of the evening.

Taylor had a huge size and strength advantage over Edwards, but it didn't stop the lightweight from sticking and moving and gamely trading blows with the heavyweight. When the 18th round began Taylor still looked fresh, while Edwards, although very plucky, looked considerably worn and used up. Edwards opened the round very spiritedly by getting in a light blow on Taylor, and the latter retaliated by knocking him prostrate with a full shoulder blow. Edwards, apparently badly shattered, came up briskly once more. The excitement at this point was intense. The combatants, with fists clenched and eyes glaring fiercely, were slowly approaching each other, glaring like tigers in their ferocity. Their respective supporters stood upon chairs and benches, shouting to them words of encouragement at the top of their lungs, creating a great uproar. The throng surged against the ropes, and Mike Coburn, a local fighter who had created a scene at the opening of the contest by challenging Edwards, decided to jump into the ring again. Amid loud outcries, whistles and catcalls, three of Edward's men dragged Coburn out of the ring, and Taylor and Edwards were about to spring forward to renew the struggle, when the proceedings degenerated to a point that a riot seemed imminent. Superintendent Campbell, who was seated on the stage, said it was time for the thing to stop. The Superintendent, Inspector Waddy, the uniformed detail, and the detective squad immediately sprang into the ring, which by this time was surrounded by a howling mob. In the excitement Taylor and Edwards clinched and their friends formed a barrier around them in an effort to screen them from the police. Superintendent Campbell made his way through the throng and ordered the combatants to clear the ring. A general and very animated scuffle at once ensued. No blows were stuck, but the cops for a moment were bundled in a completely defensive position. The uniforms and detectives held well together and shoulder to shoulder fought back the crowd. One big loafer, who attempted to assault the Superintendent, was unceremoniously thrown over the ropes by Detectives Zundt and Corwin. The boxers hastened from the ring to their dressing room. Simultaneous with their disappearance the excitement subsided, and the crowd dispersed. A few lingered about in the hope of getting a look at Edwards and Taylor.

The referee decided that the contest was a draw. Sporting men did not think that the men would meet again in the ring because Taylor was far too heavy for Edwards to handle. Owing to the near riot at the end of the bout Superintendent Campbell declared there would be no further pugilistic exhibitions at the rink.[34]

CHAPTER 11: ON THE MARK

Samuel Woodruff didn't plan on settling in Brooklyn. In fact, he didn't plan on settling anywhere. Woodruff and his wife were gypsies and lived their lives on the road, but when Mrs. Woodruff was stricken ill, Samuel Woodruff had to put down temporary roots to allow his wife time to recuperate. Woodruff set up camp opposite Phillips' Ale House on the Old Clove Road. He made the acquaintance of the Phillips', who kept a sort of public house, and he rented a room from them for his wife's occupancy during her illness. He not only rented the room, but he engaged Mrs. Phillips as a nurse, who attended to Mrs. Woodruff through her illness. Both Mr. and Mrs. Phillips were so kind that Mr. and Mrs. Woodruff appreciated them highly for it.

Woodruff was a man who had travelled over the greater part of the American continent, and by shrewd bargaining and thrifty habits succeeded in getting together about $3,000 in cash and valuables. He had been staying opposite Phillips' house for about two months, and naturally, on account of their kindness to his wife, he became friendly and familiar with them. And so, it turned out that the Phillips' not only became possessed of the knowledge that Woodruff had this money, but they also discovered its exact location in the gypsy tent. One morning, Mr. Woodruff woke up and found his money and jewelry gone. The valuables were all wrapped up in a red shawl, and the shawl and everything inside it were gone. The Woodruff's did not even have money enough left for them to buy a loaf of bread. They knew that no one but the Phillips' knew of the whereabouts of their money, and yet they could not bring themselves to believe that they were the thieves.

In despair they reported the case to the police and Detective Zundt was detailed to the case. Zundt questioned Mr. and Mrs. Phillips, but they both denied any knowledge of the theft. Zundt then obtained a search warrant and searched Phillips' house. Stuffed away under the bed, the detective found four ten-dollar bills. Mrs. Phillips claimed this was her own money, but the fact was that a week earlier they had been so hard up for money they had to borrow ten dollars from Mr. Woodruff.

The break in the case came when Detective Zundt asked the Woodruff's if there was any way they would be able to positively identify their property. Mr. Woodruff shook his head and said that he could describe his jewelry in detail, but he was not sure how he would be able to prove a specific piece of jewelry was his. Mrs. Phillips then very nonchalantly said that she had placed a mark on all their money. Zundt recoiled and wanted to make sure he had heard her correctly. "You made a mark on your money?" he asked.

"On every bill," Mrs. Woodruff nodded.

In carrying out his investigation, Zundt had discovered that Mr. Phillips had been seen the day before paying a blacksmith for repairing his wagon. The detective hurried to the Blacksmith's shop and asked to see the money he had on hand. Sure enough, a ten-dollar bill contained Mrs. Woodruff's mark. Zundt returned to the Phillips' home and asked to see the ten-dollar bills found under the bed again. His re-examination revealed that these bills also had Mrs. Woodruff's mark.

Mr. Phillips remained indignant when he was arrested and charged. After spending a night in jail, however, he became frightened at the prospect of spending a much longer period in prison, so he confessed, pulling out $730 in bills out of the toes of his shoes. This money was handed over to the police. Philips then said that the rest of the money had been buried by him. Following Phillips' directions, Zundt travelled to a potato field about a mile from the Phillips' home. He searched the fence until he came to a top rail that had been marked with a knife, just as Phillips had described. Jumping over the fence he proceeded a little distance until he came to a spot between two trees, and there he saw where the earth had been freshly turned up. Zundt dug down about a foot and struck the red shawl. He pulled up the shawl and found it to contain an assortment of jewelry and $780 in cash.

Everything was brought to police headquarters and in taking an inventory of all the property and money recovered, Detective Zundt found that there was still $799 missing. Zundt believed Phillips had hidden the missing money at another location, and that at some point his wife would be able to retrieve it. Emily Phillips had not pled guilty like her husband and demanded a separate trial because she claimed she was not aware of her husband's crime. Mrs. Phillips got her separate trial but was ultimately convicted of the theft. If the missing money was buried at another location, it would be a long time before either of the Phillips' could dig it up.[35]

CHAPTER 12: SLEEP AT YOUR OWN RISK

On a beautiful Saturday afternoon, Patrick McLaughlin, a former clerk in the Tax Office, and well-known Brooklynite, went to Myrtle Avenue Park, to attend a picnic of the Kings County Branch of Saint Patrick's Mutual Alliance. The day was warm and after exercising for some time, Mr. McLaughlin selected a shady nook in which he found a bench sheltered by the spreading branches of a large tree. Here Mr. McLaughlin sat down and, finding that he was not likely to be disturbed, he stretched himself at full length on the rustic seat and dozed off to sleep.

When he awoke the stars had come forth and the throng who were sporting in the park when he lay down had taken themselves to the dancing platform. The hour seemed late, and instinctively, Mr. McLaughlin's hand journeyed in the direction of his watch pocket, in search of his time peace, but the pocket was empty. It took a very short time for reality to set in that he had been robbed, and he proceeded to take an inventory of himself. His diamond pin and $85 in cash were also gone. Mr. McLaughlin immediately travelled to the Ninth Sub-Precinct station and reported the theft to the desk sergeant.

But there was no clue to the thieves, and it remained only to inform the detectives and trust their skill. Fortunately for Mr. McLaughlin, Detective George Zundt took on the case. Zundt realized that events with crowds of people drew thieves like moths drawn to flames. Earlier in the day he had walked around the park to see if he could spot any "moths." He took particular note of a young man named John Foley, who lived on Kosciusko Street. Although only twenty-two years of age Foley had established himself as a first-class thief.

After Zundt completed his interview with McLaughlin, he immediately headed for Kosciusko Street. It only took a short period of interrogation before Foley folded and admitted to participating in the theft. He admitted taking the watch, which McLaughlin valued at $175, and selling it to Joseph Finken, of DeKalb Avenue for $20.

Foley also admitted that his accomplice at the park was John Hanovan. Detective Zundt also knew Hanovan, who came from a respectable family, but had disgraced himself by stealing horses.

The next day Zundt arrested Finken for receiving stolen goods, and then set out to find John Hanovan. He found him selling tickets at Jewell's Wharf, to those about to start on the excursion of the Henry Corr Association. He was dressed to kill, in new clothes purchased with Mr. McLaughlin's money. A young lady was standing near him, ready to take his arm when he completed his duties as ticket seller. Detective Zundt spoiled his day's enjoyment by inviting his attention to more pressing business, like a trip to jail.[36]

CHAPTER 13: BOYS WILL BE BOYS

George Zundt had looked forward to the Friday in August when the third police picnic of the season took place at Peter A. Tilyou's Surf House on Coney Island. Zundt finally had the chance to spend some leisure time with one hundred and fifty of his brother officers and their families. He also appreciated being able to spend some quality time with his wife and children.

The event was being enjoyed by all, but as the afternoon wore on and the hot sun combined with the free flow of beer and liquor, some of the fellows became a bit raucous and several fights sprung up in different areas of the picnic.

Not too far from Zundt and his family, Sergeant Maher, of the Eighth Sub-Precinct, was enjoying the picnic with his family on the platform of the Surf House. Zundt suddenly turned toward the Maher family when he heard voices that did not sound like a family enjoying a picnic. Zundt observed that Officers McCauley and Campbell, who appeared very drunk, were very boisterously threatening to "lick" Sergeant Maher. McCauley slurred something about the sergeant trying to get him dismissed from the force a couple of years earlier. Zundt heard the sergeant deny the allegation, and then McCauley threatened to punch the sergeant.

Sergeant Maher warned McCauley not to hit him, but then Campbell joined the dispute and told McCauley to go ahead and punch the big-headed son of a bitch. McCauley then said he wanted to profit from the engagement and that he would beat up the sergeant for $100.

Detective William Folk was sitting about twenty feet from Zundt. As the dispute threatened to spin out of control, Folk and Zundt exchanged nods and waded into the middle of the problem.

Detective Folk pulled Campbell away while asking him if he was anxious to lose his job, and to stop using vulgar language around the families. Sergeant Maher had also been yelling, and Folk respectfully reminded the sergeant that he should behave appropriately for his rank. Detective Zundt pulled McCauley from the fray and told him to cool down for his own good.

The matter came to the notice of the police commissioners through newspapers the next morning, and the board at once ordered Inspector Waddy (who was present at Coney Island) to subpoena all persons who witnessed the affair and to see that charges were preferred against all guilty parties. Eight charges were preferred, including charges of "gross misconduct and using threatening and abusive language to a superior officer" against officers McCauley and Campbell. In the end, nothing serious came of the charges and Detective Zundt found himself back in the calmer environment of detective work.[37]

CHAPTER 14: INTER-CITY COOPERATION?

During December 1876, six masked men went to the Sunswick House, kept by William H. Green, in Astoria, in Queens County, and presenting pistols at the head of the residents, drove them all into one room, and then kept them there while others of the gang separated and ransacked the house. They then went to the house of Mr. H.L. Hiller, in Ravenswood, and stole over $2,000 worth of jewelry and clothing. They proceeded in just the same manner that they had done at Green's house. While the police of Long Island City were looking for the men who had robbed Green's house, the robbers themselves were busy at work at Hiller's house, which was within a stone's throw of the Long Island City Police headquarters.

These crimes were huge news, not only in Long Island City, but also in New York and Brooklyn. Ever since the robbery the Long Island City Police were hard at work trying to arrest the robbers or get some clue, but they were unsuccessful until three days after the crime, when Officer Maher, of the Long Island City Police Department, had a conversation with a man who knew more than he should have about the robbery. Maher had previously heard that the man had been talking about the robbery and approached him on the subject. The man told Officer Maher that on the second day after the crime he met a man named John Connors, who lived in South Brooklyn.

Connors asked the man, "Is there anything new about the Astoria robbery?"

The man replied, "Not that I know of."

"Do you think," asked Connors, "that the police are on the right track?"

The man shrugged. "I can't say. I don't see anything except what is said in the papers."

"Well," continued Connors, "I was in that."

"Is that so?"

"Yes – but don't you give me away."

The man promised he would say nothing, and then he alleged Connors told hm that he was one of the six men that had landed in Astoria with a boat and after robbing the houses returned to the boat and rowed back to Brooklyn. On the return trip, Connors said the thieves fought over the spoils, and Connors showed a scratch on his face he received during a fight. He also showed a gold watch and chain which had been stolen from Mr. Hiller, and he finished up by asking the man to let him know if he found out that the Long Island City Police were on the right track.

The informant, however, got drunk, and since the robbery was the all absorbing question of the day, it was discussed in the barroom where he was drinking, and he let out the principal facts of the case, and the information soon reached the ear of Officer Maher.

Acting on the information, Officer Maher chose not to notify his boss, Captain Woods of the Long Island City Police, but instead went to Superintendent Campbell of the Brooklyn Police Department. Maher told the Superintendent that he wanted to arrest Connors and requested assistance from the Brooklyn Police Department. Campbell sent Maher at once to Captain P.H. Leavy, of the Third Precinct, and he assigned Detective Mahoney to find John Connors. Mahoney arrested him the next morning on Hamilton Avenue, near the ferry, and locked him up in the Third Precinct. Superintendent Campbell then telegraphed Officer Maher to come to take his prisoner. Officer Maher, accompanied by Officer Lang arrived at the Third Precinct and were immediately convinced the prisoner was not the man they were looking for. The informant had told Maher that Connor's face and body was covered with smallpox pock marks, and that his face was scratched from the fight on the boat after the robbery. The prisoner had none of these marks. The prisoner had accounted for his time all day Friday and Saturday, and detective Mahoney, by thoroughly investigating the case, found that his wife and other parties confirmed his story. Still, the name, resemblance, and occupation of the man was so close that

Captain Leavy decided not to give him up until the officers brought the informant face to face with him and said whether or not Connors was the man.

The two Long Island City policemen started off in the early afternoon to get the informant and bring him to the Third Precinct. When the informant arrived, he confirmed that the prisoner was not the man who had bragged about the crime in the barroom.

Superintendent Campbell put Detective Zundt on the case, and he worked feverishly to solve the mystery. His major problem, however, was the insolent treatment he received from the Long Island City Police Department. Specifically, Captain Woods was miffed that he had not been brought into the investigation immediately, so he refused to aid the Brooklyn detective, and was even being untruthful to Zundt's questions about the case.[38]

Detective Zundt ignored Captain Woods' obstructionist tactics, and instead traveled across the river to work with Captain Murray, of the New York City Police Department's Fourth Precinct. Captain Murray had received reliable information from a source he would not identify regarding the identities of the robbers. Following a brief follow-up investigation, Detective Zundt and his NYPD colleagues arrested John Roberts, James "Fatty" Farrell, James McCarty, James "Juggy" Riley, and John Schmidt.

The first clue Captain Murray obtained was when his source gave him a gold pencil case that was given to him by "Fatty" Farrell, who said it came from the house robberies. The Captain then went to work with his own Detective Carr and Brooklyn's Detective Zundt. Roberts and Farrell lived in Brooklyn while the rest of the crooks resided in Manhattan. Captain Murray decided that the arrests should be made simultaneously, so he and Zundt, along with a squad of Brooklyn detectives raided the Brooklyn homes of Roberts and Farrell, while NYPD detectives rounded up the Manhattan crooks.

Roberts' father-in-law was a German named Mr. Stork. He came home during the arrest of Roberts and Detective Zundt engaged him in conversation in German. Zundt was able to learn that John Schmidt, who lived on Cherry Street in Manhattan, was the leader of the gang that committed the robberies.

When all the arrests had been made Captain Murray, along with the New York and Brooklyn Detectives transported the prisoners to Long Island City and brought them before Justice George Parsell's court. Captain Murray produced a silk handkerchief, a pair of ladies lined dog skin gloves, two pearl handled pocket knives and an ivory handled one. These articles were all identified by Mrs. Green and Mr. and Mrs. Hiller, and additionally, Mr. Miller identified James McCarty.

As the prisoners were taken to their cells, Captain Woods stewed silently in the corner of the courtroom. As he departed, Detective Zundt turned toward Woods and nodded. "It was nice working with you, Captain."

Woods face turned a dark shade of red and he began to shake as Zundt accelerated his pace out of the courtroom and back to Brooklyn.[39]

CHAPTER 15: THE SPOILS OF WAR

On a sunny afternoon a smiling man named Thomas Byer entered the Court Street tailor shop of Mr. Conrad Beck. He displayed several fancy articles for sale and finally produced a roll of cloth which he offered at an unusually low price to Beck, who finally bought the cloth. The "agent" as Byer called himself, snapped the catch of his valise and departed. Just after he had gone, Beck found he had been robbed of a fine black cloth dress coat, and he immediately suspected the agent. Mr. Beck notified Detective Zundt of the matter and gave him a description of the agent. Zundt also canvassed stores in the area and located a proprietor on Atlantic Avenue who said someone had tried to sell him a coat fitting the description of the one stolen from Beck.

The next day Byer was passing along Court Street, and Beck happened to see him. He immediately ran out of his store and on the pretense of wanting to purchase more cloth he convinced Byer to come inside his store. As soon as the agent was in the store, Beck locked the store and sent someone to find Detective Zundt. When Zundt arrived, he found an exceedingly well dressed, gentlemanly looking man confronting Beck, who appeared to be angry and nervous. Byer was cool as a cucumber.

"Mr. Zundt," said Beck, "I think this is the man who stole that coat from me on Wednesday."

Byer, walking to the detective said, "Are you a detective?"

"I am," said Zundt, displaying his shield.

"Well now, do you think it is all probable that I stole this coat?"

"That I can't say yet," replied Zundt, "but as this man accuses you of being the thief it will be my duty to assure myself of your innocence before I let you go."

"Why, certainly," said Byer, with one of his blandest smiles, "but this is so absurd."

After asking Byer for his name and address, the detective said, "Now I happen to have found out where this coat was attempted to be sold on Atlantic Avenue, so of course, if you are innocent, you will not object to going there with me."

Byer winced just a little, but said that he would go. As soon as he entered the door of the store, both the proprietor and his wife recognized Byer as the man who had tried to sell them the coat, although he tried to deny it.

Byer went to jail and Mr. Beck got his coat back. When Beck asked Zundt what he should do with the cloth he had purchased from Byer, the detective smiled and said, "Keep it." [40]

CHAPTER 16: AN UNEXPECTED GUEST

Scientific evidence and technology have become key weapons in a modern detective's fight against crime. From fingerprints to video, to DNA evidence, today's sleuths would be paralyzed without these modern methods of acquiring evidence. This wasn't always the case, however. In the 19th century there were very few scientific evidence gathering techniques, and those that were developed were usually mocked by the "old time" detectives. Such was the case with the development of photography. Many old timers scoffed at using photographs to catch crooks, but some of the younger generation of detectives, like George Zundt, saw the value in the creation of a Rogues' Gallery. For example, for many months a very handsome young man had been terrorizing the boarding houses in Brooklyn. After renting a room and producing references he would quietly slip away taking anything not nailed down from the room. His latest victim was Mrs. Ross, of 84 Henry Street, from whom the crook carried off $150 worth of property.[41]

It had only been a few years that the Rogues Gallery became a special piece of the police machinery in Brooklyn, but the choice criminal collection quickly reached extensive proportions and mid-year of 1877 there were photos of over 1,890 men and women in the gallery. The gallery was under the charge of the detective squad, and on many occasions proved a great service to the department. The key to the gallery was carefully kept by Detective William Folk, who accurately noted down the number of the picture, and everything connected with the history of the original, so far as the police had any knowledge. This included the disposition of the offender by the prosecuting authorities, so that it could be known at a moment's reference whether a particular suspected party was at large or in prison. [42]

Mrs. Ross traveled to police headquarters and described the thief to Detective Zundt. When Zundt flipped to a page that contained the photo of William F. Leet, Mrs Ross at once put her finger on Leet's photograph, saying that it resembled the man named Kranz, who had stolen her property. The photo Mrs. Ross had identified was taken in 1871. Since William Leet was no stranger to the police photographer, Zundt pulled out a photo of Leet taken in 1876 after he was arrested for robbing a boarding house on Halsey Street. When shown the more recent photo Mrs. Ross began nodding quickly, saying that the photo was absolutely the man she knew as Kranz. Zundt now knew the man he was looking for, but after a week he was having no luck in locating William Leet.

One evening Zundt was sitting in the detective squad room in police headquarters with Detective William Folk when a man entered and said he had an appointment to see Sergeant Van Wagner. Folk casually said that Van Wagner wasn't in, but when Zundt glanced up at the man he nearly fell out of his chair. He was looking at William Leet. Zundt jumped into the conversation and explained to the man that he should wait because Van Wagner was expected back very soon. He was then able to get Folk aside to explain who the man was, and to send someone to bring Mrs. Ross to headquarters as soon as possible.

As soon as Mrs. Ross entered the room, she took a look at Leet and said, "That's him."

William Leet maintained his composure as he reached for the woman's hand. "How do you do? I don't know you."

Detective Zundt then informed Leet what he was being arrested for, making him very angry. He asked how anyone could believe that he would fall into a silly trap like this if he was, in fact, guilty. Leet then gave his age as twenty-nine and refused to say anything else.

Leet was a sharp and shrewd young man, but he did fall into a silly trap – a trap that landed him in prison for four years and was all made possible by a photograph. [43]

CHAPTER 17: RIGHT OF WAY

A riot was expected at the intersection of the Coney Island Railroad and the new line which extended from Sea Beach to Canarsie. At noon the Sea Beach and New York men had laid their track from Coney Island up to ex-Mayor Gunther's road and were ready to cross his track. Right beside Gunther's road ran the old Greenwood and Bath Plank Road, and while the courts had decided that the New York and Sea Beach Road could cross Gunther's track, it did not give them permission to pass over the Plank Road, the franchise of which Gunther owned. As soon as they attempted to run their track across the Plank Road, Mr. Gunther objected, and told Mr. Beard, the contractor, to stop work. Beard refused to do so, saying he had a right to cross.

"You can cross my track," said Gunther, "but not the Plank Road."

"We'll cross anyway," replied Beard, and at his order the gang of men went to work.

Mr. Gunther went right back to his depot and got about twenty men. With these he returned to the crossing and ordered them to prevent Beard's men from proceeding any further. The workmen jumped off the engine and armed with pickaxes and crowbars, they pushed back the rails that Beard's men had laid almost across the plank road and nearly up to the track. As soon as Beard saw this, he summoned all his men together and told them to hold on to their ground and see that the tracks were not torn up. He then told Gunther to call his men off, which the latter refused to do. After an hour's standoff, Beard's men, seeing that they outnumbered Gunther's crew, intimated they were ready to clean Gunther and his men out of the area. Gunther and Beard exchanged hot and angry words, and matters got to such a pitch that Gunther was afraid blood would be spilled. He therefore came back to Brooklyn and drove at full speed to police headquarters and informed the Superintendent. The result was that in half an hour there were reserve policemen from several precincts under the command of Captain John Mackellar of the Eighth Precinct. Assisting the captain were several detectives, including George Zundt.

The train which carried the police to the scene arrived at about three o'clock. Just as the police detained, the two gangs of men were about to fight. Crowbars were raised and some had stones when Captain Mackellar hurried his men into position and was able to prevent the brawl. Michael Cropsey, a Justice of the Peace for the town of New Utrecht, and a member of the family for which Cropsey Avenue would be named, was present in a long rubber coat and a white hat. He was counsel for the New York and Sea beach railroad and was there in the interest of the company. He became very excited when Captain Mackellar arrived, and wanted to know by what authority he was preventing his men from working.

"I am here to prevent any breach of the peace," said the captain, "and not to stop men from working."

At that time, New Utrecht was still an independent town, and not part of Brooklyn, and the justice of the peace wanted to make sure Mackellar knew it. "Well, I'm a Justice of the Peace for this town. I want you to know," said Cropsey, "and you are not in Brooklyn now. You are under my control."

The men on Cropsey's side gave a cheer and thought that the starch was taken out of the police. They were about to renew their attempt to lay the track, but Captain Mackellar shouted, "Now, you men have to understand one thing. If there's any fighting here, I'll lock up the man or men who strike a blow."

"You've got no business here," said Cropsey.

"I know my business here," retorted the captain. "I'm here to prevent any disturbance, and if you strike anyone, I'll lock you up, too."

Justice Cropsey winced under this, but he saw that Mackellar was determined, so he backed off. Coming over to Mackellar, he said meekly, "See here, Captain, I don't want to have any trouble here. We've got the right to cross, and we don't want to be interrupted. See, here are the papers from the court."

At this point, ex-Mayor Gunther joined the conversation. "That's alright. I am not objecting to your crossing the track, but you have no right to go over the Plank Road – I own it and you have no right to cross it."

Cropsey directed his response to Captain Mackellar. "Captain, we have a perfect right to cross the Plank Road. Here is the written permission of the Commissioners of Highways. The Plank Road does not belong to Gunther now, he has abandoned it and torn all the planks up. Consequently, it belongs to the town, and we have the permission of the commissioners to cross."

"Well, I have nothing to do with your quarrel," said Mackellar. "I am here to prevent fighting and I'll do it."

The police then spread themselves around and the laborers on both sides went to work, some to lay down the rails and the others to tear them up. Just where the new line was laid over the Plank Road, the company had to lay planks between their rails so that the track could easily be passed by wagons. Gunther's men went for those planks and tried to tear them up preparatory to ripping up the ties so that they could loosen the rails. Beard gathered all his men around him, and placed them on the planking, and in addition they were instructed to knock away the pickaxes and crowbars used by Gunther's men in their attempts to destroy the track. Every now and then a laborer would receive a stinging blow to the face, but the crowd was so dense the assailant could not be identified. At last Justice Cropsey sent for the manure wagon and told the men to drive up the Plank Road and stop on the crossing of the New York and Sea Beach Railroad. As soon as the workmen saw the wagon coming, they had to desist their efforts and let it pass, for it was against the law to obstruct the highway. Consequently, the wagon was driven slowly up and the workmen on either side were watching their chance to get the best of each other as soon as the wagon should pass. But as soon as the vehicle got square on the crossing – that is, on the planking between the rails – one or two of the New York and Sea Beach men, who had been previously posted, slipped a heavy chain around the wheels, and in a couple of seconds the wagon was chained firmly to the rails.

As soon as it was done and Gunther's superintendent saw it, he was furious. "Get the damn wagon out of there, boys," he shouted, and his men went right to work to do it, but while they pushed on one side, contractor Beard's men pushed on the other side, and also jumped in the wagon to make it more difficult to move.

This was an exciting time. For over four hours Gunther's men tried to get the wagon off but could not. Finally, Gunther sent down word for a man to start up in a buggy from his stable and drive along the Plank Road, so that Cropsey would have to take his wagon off. But Cropsey said he'd be damned if he'd move out of the way for Gunther's buggy, and he didn't. Several times during the wagon siege blows were struck, but the police were always prompt and checked hostilities before they got to violence. Once Cropsey, when Gunther's men had gained a point, ran in among them and made as though he would strike one of them. In an instant, he was unceremoniously yanked out of the crowd by Detective Zundt, who said, "Don't you strike that man or I'll lock you up." The Justice looked daggers, but he was wise enough not to repeat his attempt, much less carry it out.

The standoff continued until nine o'clock, when Justice A.T. Carpenter, of New Utrecht arrived on a special train. He carried with him an injunction signed by Judge Gilbert, restraining the Sea Beach men from working or doing anything further as far as the Plank Road was concerned, until there could be a hearing on the matter. Both sides dispersed and Detective Zundt could cease his riot control duties and get back to detective work.[44]

CHAPTER 18: A REUNION WITH OLD FRIENDS

Charles Gastenburg was tired of trying to make a living operating his grocery and liquor store, so he made up his mind to sell his business. He became acquainted with Mr. George Pendergast, who had a real estate and coal office on the corner of 29th Street and Broadway in Manhattan, and who said he was interested in buying Gastenburg's business. Gastenburg asked $1,900 for his store, stock, fixtures, and a horse and wagon, and Pendergast did not dispute the price. Pendergast said that he did not have ready cash, but represented to Gastenburg that he was the owner of eighteen desirable lots in Newark and would give him six of them for his store. Gastenburg thought over the matter and finally agreed to accept the offer. He signed over the deed of his store to Pendergast, and the latter gave Gastenburg deeds to the Newark properties.

Five months after the transaction took place Gastenburg started off to Newark to see his properties. Pendergast had a friend named Ferguson, who was a Manhattan lawyer. When Gastenburg went to the Register's Office in Newark, Pendergast arranged for Ferguson to be there, and to meet Gastenburg as if by chance. When Gastenburg said that he called at the Register's office to learn if the deeds which he held were alright, Ferguson told him that he had already made a search, and that they were correct, and there was no need for Gastenburg to go through the expense of having another search made. Gastenburg was in doubt, but all his doubts were removed when Ferguson offered to show him the properties. The lawyer showed Gastenburg six lots, whose descriptions agreed with those given on the deeds, and Gastenburg was well satisfied with what he believed to be his property.

Sometime after he had exchanged his store for Pendergast's lots, Gastenburg went into another business, and being hard pressed for money, gave a creditor two promissory notes, showing him the deeds of the lots in Newark. The new business was not profitable, and when the notes became due Gastenburg was unable to pay. His creditor was about to take his Newark lots, but when he visited the Register's Office in Newark, he found that Gastenburg did not own the property. This information was communicated to Gastenburg, and a search of the records in the Register's Office revealed the fact that Pendergast had never owned the property, so Gastenburg took out a warrant for his arrest.

The complainant's story was so peculiar that it was deemed advisable to give the case special attention, and accordingly, the arrest warrant was placed in the hands of Detective Zundt. Zundt's investigation quickly revealed that Pendergast was an accomplished swindler, and other cases in which he obtained money under false pretenses came to light. When Gastenburg's store came into the possession of Pendergast, the latter got a mortgage on it for $900 and then gave it up.

It turned out that a favorite mode of his to swindle unsuspecting persons was to insert an advertisement for a partner, with a small capital investment, offering large returns. In most cases his victims swallowed the bait thrown out to them by the swindler and he quickly fleeced them. He also advertised for bookkeepers and confidential clerks, in all cases requiring that the party who wished the position should deposit a few hundred dollars with him as security, promising to pay it back as soon as the clerk proved himself to be honest and capable. Mr. Pendergast never had a clerk that proved to be honest and capable, or if they did it was not down on his program to return their deposit in full if at all.

In partnership with a man named Collins, Pendergast opened a hotel in Rockaway a few years earlier. The speculation was not a good one, and the pair wishing to make up for their losses, advertised for a man to take charge of their bathing houses, offering a large salary. It was required of the successful applicant for the position that he should deposit $250 with the proprietors. They said he would have the care of valuables in his position as keeper of the bath houses, and they wanted some security as they would be held accountable for his actions. Two days later after the man deposited $250 with Pendergast & Collins, they were sold out by the Sheriff of Queens County, and the keeper of their bathing houses lost the money which he had deposited with them.

Zundt had surprisingly little trouble finding Pendergast and taking him into custody. On the morning the 26-year-old was brought before Justice Walsh to plead not guilty, word of his arrest had gotten around, and the courtroom was filled with his prior victims, all crying for his blood. It turned out the safest place for Pendergast was jail.[45

CHAPTER 19: THE GOLD WATCH

Mr. Thomas Dolan was the night superintendent of the Western Union Telegraph Company. It was a good job, but this career played a secondary role in his life. Thomas Dolan was one of the best known and most highly respected experts in horse flesh in the country and was a conspicuous figure at all leading races. His opinions were much sought after and his judgement on racing matters considered second to none. He corresponded on sporting matters with the leading metropolitan newspapers and was always regarded as a square and brilliant chronicler of turf events. A year earlier, he had been given a gold watch by some leading figures in the racing industry. The beautifully made watch was worth at least $500 but Dolan would not have parted with it for twice that amount.

While strolling along the Coney Island beach on a Saturday afternoon, Dolan became friendly with James Fuller and John McCaffrey, and as the afternoon turned into evening, his two new friends invited Dolan to Ward's Hotel to attend a raffle for a clock. There was a huge crowd in the room where the raffle was taking place, and when the winner of the clock was announced, Dolan noticed that his new friends were gone – along with his precious watch.

The following day Jimmie Elliot, a Coney Island special officer, arrested Fuller in the Atlantic Garden, but could find no trace of Dolan's watch. Dolan identified Fuller as one of the men who had robbed him, and Fuller was committed to jail. Although it was known beyond doubt that Fuller had disposed of the watch in some way in New York, Fuller refused to give the police any information which might lead to the recovery. Detective Maroney, of New York's Third Precinct was put on the case, but failed miserably to develop any information regarding the whereabouts of the watch. Mr. Dolan, however, was determined to recover his watch, and worked night and day to discover clues in both New York and Brooklyn. He even employed three Pinkerton's detectives to aid in the hunt. As days passed, the prospect of success became less likely. Fuller was still not talking, and the Third Precinct detective had made no progress whatsoever. Fortunately, George Zundt had been moving on the matter. While the other detective was on a wild goose chase after Fuller's supposed confederate in the robbery, Zundt was intelligently tracking Fuller's movements from the moment Mr. Dolan's watch disappeared. He found that Fuller at a late hour on Saturday night stopped at a low-class resort on Coney Island, where a woman he passed off as his wife lived and took her with him to New York. On Monday the woman returned to Coney Island dressed in an entirely new outfit and stated that a relative of hers had died and left her some money. Detective Zundt, as soon as he received this information, made this woman the special object of his attention, and by shrewd work managed to force a confession from her to the effect that Fuller had stolen a watch on Saturday night, and had gone to New York on Sunday to dispose of it. She positively denied, however, that she knew where the watch was.

Zundt immediately communicated with Superintendent Campbell, and the woman was arrested and brought to Brooklyn on Wednesday afternoon. There were two courses presented to her, to go to jail or to prevail upon Fuller to tell where the watch could be found. She promised, if given the opportunity to communicate with Fuller, that she would learn the location of the watch. Detective Zundt escorted the woman to the Raymond Street Jail and after a brief interview with the prisoner, she whispered to Zundt, causing the detective to depart the jail in a highly jubilant mood.

The next morning Zundt traveled to New York and stopped at the loan office of John McDuff on Bleecker Street. McDuff had advanced Fuller $100 on the watch, promising to repay $125 when he returned for the watch. McDuff refused to give up the watch to Zundt without receiving his $100, but when he accompanied Zundt to New York police headquarters, Superintendent Walling informed him he would have to surrender the watch to Zundt and look for his money at a later time. At 5 P.M. Zundt entered Superintendent Campbell's office where Mr. Dolan was sitting with the Superintendent. Dolan nearly fell out of his chair when Zundt pressed the precious watch into Dolan's hand.[46]

CHAPTER 20: THE PIRATES OF FLUSHING BAY

Nothing seemed out of the ordinary on that hot summer day in July, when young Myrtle Avenue grocer Isaac Treadwell attempted to beat the heat with a day of boating on Flushing Bay. He told friends he also intended on jumping off the boat to bathe in the bay. The next morning, however, an empty boat, with Treadwell's clothes aboard, containing a gold watch and chain, and $200 in cash, was found adrift near the Westershire shore, and as there were no traces of the young man it was supposed that he had drowned while bathing.

Three months later the community was astounded when Treadwell appeared in a robust state of health and related the most extraordinary and apparently incredible story of his disappearance.

Treadwell said that while he was cooling himself off in Flushing Bay, a small sailboat came alongside him and two men who were aboard of it dragged him out of the water, put his head in a bag and kept him a prisoner until the following morning, when he was landed at Jersey City, and compelled him under threat of murder, to board a train for Baltimore, which he reached in a half dazed condition in good time. When his mental equilibrium was somewhat restored, he sent a letter to a young lady to whom he was engaged to be married, requesting her to communicate with his relatives and to have sufficient funds forwarded to him to enable him to return home.

In a few days he received a cool response from his fiancé, advising him to stay where he was, as no one wanted him in Brooklyn. He said he was so depressed at this strange exhibition of empathy on the part of the young lady, that he became thoroughly despondent and resolved to become a wanderer on the face of the earth and to never return to his home. Sometime afterward, while in St. Louis, Treadwell said he accidentally crossed the path of an old Brooklyn friend, and through his solicitation changed his melancholy resolution.

When Treadwell returned to Brooklyn the police now had a kidnapping case to solve and Superintendent Campbell detailed

Detective Zundt to work up the case, and, if possible, secure the men who were guilty of abducting Treadwell from Flushing Bay. It was not long before Zundt discovered that there was considerable fiction, to say the least, about the story, but Treadwell was so persistent in maintaining that it was absolutely true in all its astonishing details, that he hesitated to make a final report on the matter until he could satisfy his superior officers that his first impressions were correct. Zundt completed his investigation with the result that he could discover no facts that would go to prove that Treadwell was either captured or abducted. He did, however, uncover some very curious facts. A few days after his disappearance, when he pretended to be in Baltimore, Treadwell was actually in Brooklyn, and even visited his home without the knowledge of his father. From time to time, he was also seen in New York. [47] He was missing for nearly six weeks, during which time Zundt ascertained by skillful detective ingenuity, that he had not drowned in Flushing Bay or was captured by pirates. Instead, Treadwell went on a prolonged drinking spree, which he brought to a close by enlisting in the General Mounted Service of the United States Army on September 20th. After spending a few days in New York, he was sent with a batch of recruits to Fort Jefferson Barracks, in Missouri. He seemed to have tired of the service, and without receiving leave of absence or securing his discharge, he started east and finally turned up in Brooklyn as the hero of the most remarkable yarn which had ever been attempted to be palmed off on the public.

As soon as Detective Zundt's inquiries became too unpleasantly close to revealing the truth, young Mr. Treadwell made himself scarce and again went among the missing. He was likely to remain so for some time, for some of Uncle Sam's men were after him, and were determined to capture him and return him to the Army.[48]

CHAPTER 21: ACCIDENTAL SHOOTING

Sometimes, George Zundt found a case when he least expected it. At noon Detective Zundt left police headquarters and got on a Fifth Avenue car to go home to dinner. While on Fifth Avenue, near Tenth Street, his attention was attracted by hearing his name called out loudly by a young man who was on a downtown car that was passing at the time.

Zundt recognized the young man as Frederick Lowenhagen, the bartender at Wislon's Hotel on Coney Island. Lowenhagen had jumped off the downtown car and was frantically beckoning to Zundt to get off his car. Zundt jumped out of the car and met with Lowenhagen.

"What's the matter, Fred," Zundt asked.

"Matter enough," said Lowenhagen, who was in a very excited state. "I have killed Charly Wilson and I want to give myself up."

Detective Zundt drew Lowenhagen out of traffic and asked him to explain what he just said.A n emotional Lowenhagen said, "Charly and me went out shooting this morning, in the swamp, and when I was loading my gun it went off. I don't know how it did, but it went off, and poor Charley was shot through the heart.

"Is he dead?" asked the detective.

"Oh, yes, he's dead," Lowenhagen nodded. "My God, Zundt, what will I do?"

"Did you tell his father and mother?" Zundt asked.

"No, I went back home, and they asked me where he was, and I told them he was in the swamp. I dare not tell them what had happened."

"Then I suppose we had better get right down to police headquarters," said Zundt

When Zundt and Lowenhagen arrived at headquarters, Superintendent Campbell had not come back from dinner, so while Lowenhagen was waiting, Zundt told him to tell him the complete story of what had happened.

Lowenhagen, who had become more composed than he was when he first encountered Zundt, said, "This morning, about a quarter to nine, Charly and me went out gunning. We went to the swamp where most of the people go when they want to find birds. Mr. Wilson told me to get back in time and not to stop too late for business. I said I would. The swamp is back of McPherson's place. When we got there, Charly said, 'Fred, you go up to the other end of the swamp, and I'll stay here, so if you scare any birds up there, I'll get them.' I went to the opposite end of the swamp, and in a little while I shot a couple of cat birds. I had heard Charley's gun, so I whistled for him. We have a couple of whistles to call each other. He came up, and I met him in the swamp near the cedar tree. He had shot a couple of high holders. I handed him my two cat birds, and said, 'Charly, you put them on your string.' He said, 'Alright.' While he was putting the birds on the string, I took the empty shell out of the breech of the gun. It is one of the Maynard rifles, but there are two barrels, one for shot and the other a regular rifle barrel. I had the one for shot on the stock. I don't know, for I was so excited, I could not tell whether the hammer was up or not, but I suppose it must have been. I took out the empty shell, put it in my pocket and then put in a full one. Then I took a cap out and fixed it on the shell. Just as I had done so the gun went off. Charly gave one scream and then fell back dead. He was a cripple – humpbacked – and was stooping down, as I have said. I didn't even notice at the time that the barrel of my gun was pointed in his direction. I had never had an accident before, and I never thought of such a thing. I ran to him – he was only about four or five feet from me – and I saw he was dead. I got nearly crazy. I didn't know what to do. I thought of running away as far as I could go, and then I thought about blowing my brains out. I didn't know what I was doing. At last, I picked up my gun and ran home. I got to Wilson's at about half past two. Mr. Wilson was in the bar. He said, 'Fred, you've come back early, are you through shooting?'

'Yes,' said I, 'the sun was too hot, and I don't feel well.'

'You look pale,' said Mr. Wilson to me. 'Where's Charly, is he back?'

'No,' said I, 'I left him in the swamp.'

After leaving my gun behind the bar I went out of the hotel, saying I would be back in a little while. I went to the depot and took the first train to Brooklyn. I intended to run away, but I met a friend of mine and told him the whole story. He told me that the best thing for me to do was not to run away, but to give myself up. So, I made up my mind I would come down to headquarters and give myself up to detective Zundt, you being a countryman of mine. It was when I was on the car on my way here that I met you, so I hailed you."

"You are sure that Charly was dead before you left him?" asked Zundt.

"Yes," said a crying Lowenhagen, "I was too sure."

He motioned to his heart. "He took the shot right here. All he did was give one scream and fall back. When I ran to him, I saw where the wound was, and his eyes turned all glassy like, and his tongue came out between his teeth as if he was choked."

"What was your relations with Charley – were you on good terms?"

"Oh, yes, sir. Why, I have been with Mr. Wilson for six years next June, and I was treated as kind as if I was one of the family. Why, that poor boy, I wouldn't hurt a hair on his head, nor would anyone else. If he went fishing, I always went with him. If I was going fishing or shooting, he always came with me. We always went fishing and gunning together ever since I knew him, and never had as much as a quarrel. We were like two brothers more than anyone else."

"You ought to have told Mr. Wilson about it," said one of the detectives in the room.

"I couldn't tell him. They thought so much of that boy, he was the only son, and I did, too, and I couldn't tell him. I never dare go back there anymore."

Superintendent Campbell made his appearance, and Lowehagen relayed the entire story to him.

"Then you left the body in the swamp?" Campbell asked.

"Yes, sir, just as he fell with his gun lying alongside of him."

Detective Zundt was directed to hurry to Coney Island and notify Mr. and Mrs. Wilson of what had occurred, and to make a search for the body. Lowenhagen was asked to give as near a description as he could of the location of the corpse in the swamp. He said that there was a single cedar tree near the lower end of it and that the body of the boy lay within a few feet of that. Detective Zundt started off on his mission, while Lowenhagen was detained at police headquarters to await the action of Coroner Simms, who had been notified of the case and would take charge of it as soon as Detective Zundt telegraphed the fact that the corpse had been discovered. The boy was 17 years of age while Lowenhagen was 25 years old. [49]

Zundt found the body lying on his face with a great gaping wound in the back. [50] Coroner Simms held an inquest into the facts surrounding the death of Charles S. Wilson. The principal witness was Frederick Lowenhagen, who detailed the same story he had previously told. The deceased's father and another witness testified that Lowehagen and young Wilson were on the best of terms and had been in the habit of shooting and fishing together like twin brothers. After some deliberation, the jury rendered a verdict that the deceased was accidentally shot by Frederick Lowenhagen, and the latter was exonerated from all blame in the matter. [51]

CHAPTER 22: TWO SUICIDES

Everyone in New York and Brooklyn was captivated over newspaper articles about the search for Andrew J. Gillen. The prominent New York lawyer had murdered Mary Siegerson, daughter of New York Assistant Corporation Attorney Michael H. Siegerson, presumably because Miss Siegerson had told her family that she planned on ending her relationship with Gillen. New York police could find no trace of Andrew Gillen.

Five days after the murder in Brooklyn, eleven-year-old John Freeman was in a hurry. His mother had warned him to be home at seven o'clock, and it was now five minutes past the hour, and he still had a long distance to cover to reach his Canton Street home. John took a shortcut by running through City Park. As he ran down Concord Street he paused momentarily when he heard a groan coming from a bench about one hundred and fifty yards from Navy Street, facing Flushing Avenue. He hurried to the bench and discovered that a man had apparently shot himself through the head, the ball having entered through the mouth and passing out in the region of the left ear, grazing a neighboring tree as it sped onward. The man was not yet dead, but he was unable to speak, and blood was pouring in torrents from his wound. In a few moments he fell on one side of the bench, disclosing under his overcoat the weapon with which he had committed the deed, a five-shot revolver, known as "the British Bulldog." The man's face, clothing, gun, and the bench were all covered in blood. The shocked boy ran from the scene to find a policeman.

Officer Joseph Dugan, of the Fourth Precinct, happened to be in the vicinity, and when informed of the condition wasted no time in running to the scene. A crowd had gathered around the man, who was still groaning in the most pathetic manner. The officer went to the station house to summon an ambulance. The Eastern District Ambulance responded promptly, but it was too late, as the man was dead when the surgeon took hold of his wrist and felt no pulse.

Sergeant Carpenter and three additional officers from the Fourth Precinct were on the scene, and they requested the ambulance surgeon to remove the body to the morgue. The surgeon refused to do so, saying that the ambulance was not to be degraded by being made to perform the duty of an undertaker's wagon. Accordingly, it was determined to remove the remains to the morgue on a stretcher. One was procured after considerable delay, and as the body was carried through the streets, it was followed by an immense crowd of excited men and women. The excitement was amplified by the rumor that was spreading quickly through the crowd that the suicide victim was, in fact, Andrew Gillen.

The body was placed on a marble slab in Room 5 at the morgue, and an opportunity was offered to obtain an accurate description of the suicide victim. He looked to be about 25 years old, five foot seven or eight inches in height, with light brown hair, sandy mustache, and small light chin whiskers. He had light blue eyes and was light complexioned. The police officials at the morgue agreed that the suicide victim fit the description of Andrew Gillen perfectly.

A search of the dead man's person and clothing revealed no identity papers. A fifty-cent piece and twelve pennies were found in his pockets, as were also a bunch of keys and an empty memorandum book. The police officers returned to the station house and reported to Captain Wilmarth, taking the blood-stained gun with them.

The detective squad obtained a photograph of Gillen, and when the picture was brought to the morgue, all the detectives but one believed the man on the slab to be Andrew Gillen. The lone dissenter was Detective George Zundt, who pointed out that the man had a German-looking face and the shoes he was wearing were German made. He also said that the small amount of money in his possession indicated that the dead man was a poor emigrant.

Superintendent Campbell telegraphed New York Police Superintendent Walling and several hours later New York police escorted a relative of Gillen's into the Brooklyn Morgue. This relative confirmed Detective Zundt's assessment that the body was definitely not Andrew Gillen.[52]

Andrew Gillen may not have committed suicide on that November evening in Brooklyn, but it turned out to be a premonition of his fate. On December 5th, 1880, telegraph messages were received in police headquarters in both Brooklyn and New York from the police department in Cedar Keys, Florida. Andrew Gillen had shot himself a day earlier in Cedar Keys and made a deathbed confession before he died. Gillen had declared that the shot that killed Mary Siegerson was meant for himself, and that they had been engaged to be married since 1878. Gillen said that Mary's brother was opposed to the engagement and did what he could to have their mother oppose it also. Gillen said that on the night of the murder, he had taken a drink of water and then turned to put his arm around Mary's neck, and she put her right arm around him. He said that they walked together a few steps, then he showed her a new pistol which he had. He then said he pointed the pistol at his own heart and told her that he would take his own life if he couldn't be with her. Gillen said that Mary nestled close to him, and while he was holding her the gun went off and she fell from his arms. He said he was frantic and began running for a physician, but instead went to a relative's home and stayed there for several days until the relative helped him to leave New York.[53]

CHAPTER 23: RESCUED FOR THE GALLOWS

16-year-old Barbara Grouenthal was the eldest daughter of a widow who resided on Wallabout Street. The family of German descent was poor but respectable. Barbara had recently found employment as a servant girl with the family of Mr. Charles Carlisle, of 502 Willoughby Avenue. During the short time she had been in his employ she had conducted herself in a creditable manner.

One of the acquaintances of the Grouenthal family was James Walsh. He became acquainted with Barbara and conceived an intense passion for her. His advances, however, were not reciprocated by Barbara. Walsh, however, continued to visit her house and ingratiated himself with the mother, and soon became a regular visitor to the house. When Barbara had made up her mind to go to work, she told her mother she was glad for the chance to get rid of Walsh and begged her not to inform him where she was working. The mother, however, did tell Walsh, and during her first week of employment, he called on her at the Carlisle house. His persistent attention went so far, that on New Years' Eve, when Barbara was spending the evening with her mother, Walsh was on hand to meet her and managed to remain there all night, and the next morning accompanied back to the Carlisle house, making the strange remark when departing the house that he planned on going to a wake that night.

That day Barbara stated to Mr. Carlisle's young daughter that Walsh annoyed her and that she did not want him calling upon her. She must have known he was going to call on her the next night, because when he rattled the iron gate, she ran out instantly to prevent him from coming into the house. She stood talking to him in the bitter cold for fifteen or twenty minutes. When she returned to the home, she appeared to be very angry, and once or twice she said that she wished that Walsh would never call on her again.

When it finally sank into Walsh that Barbara wanted nothing to do with him, he resolved that if he couldn't have her, no one would.

At seven o'clock Walsh was observed by some of the Carlisle neighbors hanging around the outside of the Carlisle house. At some point a man employed by Mr. Carlisle exited the house to get some coal which was kept in a bin underneath the front stoop. The man asked Barbara to hold the lamp for him until he had filled his bucket with coal. As he loaded the bucket he happened to look up and noticed Barbara staring intently toward the fence. He followed her gaze and observed a man leaning on the fence outside the property. The man gathering the coal said later that Barbara seemed upset and displeased with her observation as she followed him back into the house. The employee said that once they had entered the house, Barbara put down the lamp and then immediately went outside to speak to the man at the fence. About thirty seconds later Barbara shrieked in an agonizing voice, "Oh, I'm stabbed! I'm stabbed!"

Barbara staggered into the house and fell into the arms of one of the female members of the Carlisle family. She was bleeding from a wound just above the heart and was unable to say another word after shrieking that she had been stabbed.

The police were notified, and Dr. George H. Fuller was summoned. He arrived simultaneously with Captain McLaughlin and Detective Kelly, of the Ninth Precinct, but Barbara was already dead. In searching the area, the knife was found in a heap of snow in front of the house. It had a 4-inch blade and had been recently sharpened.

A general alarm was sent out. A description of Walsh was obtained from Barbara's mother and all stations were notified to be on the lookout. Superintendent Campbell placed several detectives on the case, including George Zundt, but as the night wore on, no clues were obtained. With no success on the case, Zundt returned to headquarters and noticed the following telegram that had arrived minutes earlier:

About 9:30 P.M. an unknown man, about twenty-two years old, five feet seven inches, fair complexion and hair, smooth face, dark clothes, derby hat, low shoes, was found in the Gowanus Canal near the Ninth Street

Bridge and was rescued by the driver and conductor of a Smith Street car. He was taken to the Long Island College Hospital.

Zundt was struck by the similarities in the description of the man pulled out of the water and James Walsh. He rushed to the hospital and quickly determined that the rescued man was, in fact, James Walsh. Detective Zundt wasted no time in extracting a full confession from Walsh. He admitted he killed Barbara, "all through love." He said that she had refused to have him and that he could not live without her.

When Walsh was discharged from the hospital Detective Zundt brought him before Superintendent Campbell at police headquarters, but Walsh whined and cried so much that he could not say another word. Zundt had to literally hold him up or Walsh would have fallen. Walsh had to be helped into Justice Walsh's court and when asked what he had to say to the crime he was charged with, he could not answer.[54]

Despite his full confession, James Walsh pleaded not guilty to murdering Barbara Grouenthal by reason of insanity. He was convicted at his trial and sentenced to hang. After almost two years of appeals and a temporary stay of execution by the governor, Walsh's sentence was affirmed and he was condemned to be hanged on July 21, 1882.

The evening before his execution, Walsh sent for his attorney, Abraham H. Dalley. "I wanted to see you before I go," said Walsh, "because you have been so kind to me."

"I only wish our labors had been rewarded with victory," said the lawyer.

"Well," Walsh said with a slight smile, "I have made up my mind that I must go tomorrow, and I feel that when the end comes, I shall go to heaven."

"I think you will," added Dalley, "for I feel satisfied that you are truly repentant."

"Yes, sir," Walsh agreed, "and as long as I've got to go, I may as well go now as at any other time.

Undersheriff Hodgkinson also visited during the evening. "Well, Jimmie, I'm sorry it has come to this, but we have to do our duty."

"Yes Mr. Hodgkinson," replied Walsh, "I know that. You and the sheriff have been very kind to me, and I hope you will both be rewarded in heaven."

Sheriff Stegman also visited Walsh. "Now Walsh, you know that you've got to go – you can't help it, my boy, and I can't. Now, I want you to face this ordeal like a soldier going to battle. You've got the advantage of a great many, Jimmie. You've had the best of religious instruction, and as I know you are sincere, I am satisfied that you have nothing to be afraid of. I want to see you brave to the last."

"Why, Mr. Stegman," replied Walsh, "I am perfectly prepared now, but so long as I do live, I want to attend to my instructions, and I am satisfied that it is better for me to go tomorrow, as God has willed that it should be so.

"That's right, Jimmie, that's the spirit you should have.

As the time of execution drew closer, Walsh bid an emotional farewell to his mother, sister and younger brother. As the relatives were being led away from the cell, his mother broke away and ran down the corridor back to the cell.

"Let me in to my boy. Let me in to my boy," she shrieked loudly. "I must be with my boy."

"Go away, mother," Walsh cried from inside the cell. "This is too much."

Walsh was extremely upset as his mother was led away. Father Donohue remained in the cell for a while until Walsh was calm, then the priest left the condemned man alone.

At 8 A.M., after a poor night's sleep, Fathers Donohue and Gallagher were let into the cell. After Walsh dressed, the priests accompanied him into another cell that was closer to the gallows. The priests remained in the cell until a few minutes before ten o'clock. At that time Undersheriff Hodgkinson entered the cell and produced the death warrant. While the warrant was being read, Walsh slumped down on the cot and cried. The priests, who were outside the cell, observed his breakdown and were allowed to return to his side.

At ten o'clock sharp the march to the gallows commenced. Walsh lost all his confidence as soon as he left the cell and had to be fully supported by a priest on either side of him. The resolution of Walsh to "die like a man," had forsaken him. He was weak and pale. But for the assistance of his religious advisors, he could not have stepped onto the gallows' platform. The assistant executioner adjusted the knot beneath Walsh's right ear, and when a signal was received from Undersheriff Hodgkinson, the knot was tightened.

"Into thy hand, oh Lord, I give my soul," said the priest.

"Into thy hand, oh Lord, I give my soul," responded Walsh.

At this point the assistant executioner pulled the black cap down over Walsh's eyes. Before it could be pulled down completely, the condemned man seemed to take in the situation. "Not yet, Father, not yet" he exclaimed.

Walsh's lips began to quiver, and he began to sway back and forth, and it was evident that he had broken down completely. While Walsh was still trembling like a leaf, the sheriff removed his handkerchief from his pocket, the pre-ordained signal to the executioner.

"Thud, thud," was heard, and Walsh's body sprung eight feet into the air. At 10:17 Walsh was declared dead and at 10:34 the body was lowered into a mahogany coffin, which bore the inscription:

James F. Walsh, Died July 21, 1882, Aged 19 years and 5 months

James Walsh's final thoughts as the rope was being tightened around his neck was likely a wish that those good Samaritans had never pulled him out of the Gowanus Canal almost two years earlier.[55]

CHAPTER 24: FAMILY AFFAIRS

Frank Van Ness seemed to be living the American Dream. The 29-year-old was married to his wife Frances for nine years, he had a good job as an accountant and lived in a nice home on St. James Place in Brooklyn. Then, one day, Frank disappeared.

Frances Van Ness and the children were very worried. Mrs. Van Ness travelled to Manhattan to Frank's place of employment, E.W. Hartwell and Company, on West 23rd Street, where she was told that Frank was still employed by the business, but that he had not been at work for a couple of days. A day later Frances was confused when another person who worked for the company stopped by her home and mentioned that Frank had not missed a day at work. Frances decided to go back to West 23rd Street and covertly watch the building where her husband worked. It didn't take long before she observed her husband leave the building and enter a dining saloon further down West 23rd Street.

When Frances entered the establishment, she was stunned to see Frank sit at a reserved table already occupied by a beautiful, young Hispanic woman, and order dinner. While battling to control her growing rage, Frances watched the couple, and observed frequent acts of endearment which passed between them. Unable to remain a silent witness to the spectacle any longer, Frances walked over and stood next to the table occupied by her husband.

For an instant, Frank showed no reaction to the presence of his wife. The woman, who was identified as Miss Lila Velese, was just as calm. The air of tranquility burst with the barrage of epithets Frances rained on Lila, to which Lila responded in kind.

"You have my husband, you minx!" were Mrs. Van Ness' parting words, "and I want you to give him up to me."

"I am not keeping him," retorted Lila. "He can go now if he wants to. I can pay for what I have eaten."

Frank Van Ness did not miss his opportunity. By the time the two women looked for his input he had already "skipped" out of the restaurant, leaving the two women to fight it out alone. Lila settled the bill and departed with her clothes intact and none of her hair missing.

Frank Van Ness did not return home. To the contrary, three days later on January 9th, he married Lila at her parents' residence on State Street. Despite the scene in the restaurant Van Ness told Lila and her family that he was a single man and was able to marry Lila. He gave Lila's brother the address of his employer, who, he stated, would give him a reference. What Lila's family didn't know was that Van Ness had gone to his boss, Mr. Hartwell, informed him of the trouble he had gotten into, and begged him to tell anyone who came inquiring that he was single. Lila's brother was satisfied when he met Mr. Hartwell and was told that Frank Van Ness was a single man. This satisfied Lila's family, but Frank still had to explain to Lila the encounter in the restaurant. Frank swore to Lila that he was divorced from his wife, but that his wife could not accept the fact that they were no longer married.

After the wedding, Lila and Frank went to Philadelphia. Frances learned of the second marriage and procured an arrest warrant on the charge of bigamy. The warrant was entrusted to George Zunt for service. Zundt found that Van Ness and his second wife were staying in a fashionable boarding house in the City of Brotherly Love. It was eleven o'clock when Zundt rang the bell. He had discovered that Van Ness was traveling under the name Frank Wright, and when the door opened the detective said, "Is Mr. Frank Wright in?"

"Yes, sir, but he is upstairs," said an employee. "Will you wait in the parlor?"

"Oh, never mind that," said Zundt. "I've come a long way and I want to surprise him during his honeymoon. What floor is he on?"

"Front room on the second floor."

"All right," said Zundt, and up he went to the door. He knocked and Van Ness opened it. As soon as he did so Zundt forced his way into the room. Van Ness was half dressed, and Lila was smoking a cigarette. Upon the table was a pitcher of beer from which the couple had been drinking.

"What do you mean by this?" an angry Van Ness demanded.

Zundt told him about the warrant and Van Ness was considerably staggered. At first, he said he wouldn't come to Brooklyn unless he was extradited from Philadelphia, but when he found out he would be locked up in Philadelphia until the paperwork could be completed, he decided to come quietly.

Upon arriving in Brooklyn Van Ness was locked up in the Washington Street station house where he wrote a letter to Lila before he would appear in Justice Walsh's court.

My Dear, Darling, Sweetest Lila – With the iron bars before me and no longer a free man, my heart is yet free to write what is in it for you. Oh, my Lila, need I tell you that I have only one thought at the moment in all my trouble and that is the most underlying love for the little girl who stood by me so bravely when the storm came. Oh, my beloved, I beseech you to be ever as true in the future as you have been in the past. When you get home, I know what will be said to you. I know that I will be cursed and called all manner of things. I know that your people will do their utmost to turn you from me. But oh, my love! My Lila! I beg you to remember all you have promised. I know you are brave and strong. I know your love is true and pure, but I know also that you will be put to a severe test. I do not write this because I doubt for a moment that you will keep faith. I write only to warn you to be prepared for any arguments or persuasions that may be used against me by them. Do come and see me before you go, if only for a moment. Oh, my darling, I send you a thousand kisses. Pray for us and our speedy reunion.

When brought to court Justice Walsh ordered Van Ness held without bail. By the time the formal examination was to be conducted, Frank's luck began to change for the better. Before the hearing, Frances Van Ness appeared in the office of District Attorney Ridgeway with a complete change of heart. She had decided to withdraw her complaint because she realized that if her husband went to prison, there would be no support for her family. Ridgeway said he could not simply drop the case, but that he would make sure Frank received bail, and hopefully the matter could be resolved to her satisfaction at trial.

Frank Van Ness was released on bail and the big question was which wife he would run to. The answer was neither. On the date of the next court appearance, he failed to appear, and another warrant was issued for his arrest. This time he did a first-class job of "skipping," as Frank Van Ness or Frank Wright was never heard from again.[56]

On Christmas Eve 1884, a richly dressed woman sat sobbing in Justice Naeher's Brooklyn court. Her youthful and aristocratic appearance was sufficient at once to attract the attention of nearly everyone in the courtroom, but she paid no attention to the curious glances thrown her way, as her mother and brother, who sat beside her, vainly attempted to comfort her. The family was recognized as one of the more prominent in Brooklyn society, and their appearance in a police court, especially on Christmas Eve, seemed strangely out of place. On the other side of the room sat a tall, handsome, well-dressed man, about 35-years of age. Occasionally, the richly dressed woman glanced appealingly at the handsome man, but he returned her glances coldly, and she soon turned her eyes away, and broke into a fresh fit of sobbing.

The couple were husband and wife. The husband was Henry M. Abernathy, the son of a distinguished New York physician, and the wife was Louisa Hunt - Abernathy, a young lady who reigned in certain rather exclusive Brooklyn circles as a society belle. She was in court to press against her husband a charge of abandonment. The couple had two very beautiful children who were in the custody of the wife, but it was known that their father would sacrifice everything to gain custody of them.

What had brought this upscale family into the courtroom? Several months earlier Mr. Abernathy was finding it difficult to support his family as stylishly as he imagined his wife desired, so he proposed an idea. The family would move to his brother's farm in Sullivan County where he would work on the farm and the family would be comfortable and happy leading a simple, country lifestyle. This premise was used a little less than a hundred years later in a television sitcom called Green Acres, where a New York City couple moves to the country on the insistence of the husband. The move didn't work out on the television show, and it didn't work out in real life for the Abernathy's.

Mr. Abernathy moved to the farm and settled in a month before he sent for his wife and children. Farm life quickly proved to be anything but pleasant for the society woman, and angry disputes arose between Louisa, her husband, and his brother. Louisa said she was compelled alone to perform all the kitchen work for the farm hands besides attending to every other household duty, and that when she declared she was unable to do all the required work she was cruelly and even brutally treated by her husband. Mr. Abernathy said that his wife continued to act like a city woman and refused to sew even a button on his coat. After a few weeks Mrs. Abernathy returned to Brooklyn with the children, feeling that she had been driven from the farm by her husband's brutality. She believed that if he, too, would return to the city they might live happily together again, and in order to get him back to Brooklyn she swore out a warrant for his arrent on the charge of abandonment, with the document being placed in the hands of Detective Zundt for execution.

Zundt found his man on December 16th driving along a lonely road in Sullivan County and immediately took him into custody. Abernathy took a look at the warrant, saw that it was not endorsed, and declined to accompany Zundt to Brooklyn. Detective Zundt did not allow the administrative mistake to hamper him. He took Abernathy before a Sullivan County magistrate who placed him under bond to appear in Brooklyn. And so, on Christmas Eve, Henry Abernathy found him sitting in the courtroom trying to avoid his wife's sobbing eyes.

Mrs. Abernathy tried several times to talk with her husband in the courtroom, but members of the Abernathy family broke in on every attempt at conversation, and the half-frantic woman declared in desperation that her husband's family were lined up against her. Justice Naeher had a long consultation with all parties in his private room and vainly attempted to bring about a reconciliation. Abernathy said he would support his wife if she would live on the farm. The wife declared that she would rather die than do that. Mrs. Abernathy's brother said that his sister would never go back to the farm, but if Henry would move back to Brooklyn, he would support their family until Henry found a suitable job. Henry's response to the offer was only a disdainful sneer. Finally, Justice Naeher decided to hear further proceedings in open court, and the couple, a moment later, stood before the magisterial bench. An adjournment until January 16th was agreed upon, and then it was discovered that Abernathy's bail bond was about to expire and that he would have to get fresh bail.

"Oh, Harry, why can't you end this dreadful matter now?" exclaimed Louisa. "I don't ask you to support me. I only ask that you come here and make me as happy as I was before your brother interfered with us. Say you will do that, and I will withdraw the charges."

Henry Abernathy coldly murmured something about not being permitted to see his children, which caused his wife to cry, "Yes, you can see the children anytime. I would give anything to have you come to our house, where we can talk without restraint. Will you do it, Harry?"

"I will not," was the cool response.

"Well, I withdraw the charge," said Mrs. Abernathy, again bursting into tears. "I withdraw the charge, Judge Naeher, whether he wishes to support me or not. I Cannot, I cannot take any further proceedings against my husband. Let him go away from me if he wishes. I will not try again to stop him – Oh, Harry, Harry, Harry!"

The woman turned away, completely overcome with grief, while her husband still stood silent and unmoved. Her relatives tried to get Louisa to reconsider her decision, but she could not be induced to renew the charge against her husband. An hour later all parties left the courtroom, and husband and wife walked off in opposite directions, the husband headed for the next train to Sullivan County and the wife on her way to live with her mother on Adelphi Street. Detective Zundt stood on the courthouse steps and watched the couple fade away in the distance. He took a deep breath, adjusted his hat and said to no one in particular, "Merry Christmas to all, and to all a goodnight." [57]

CHAPTER 25: MURDER OR SELF-DEFENSE?

At 4:40 P.M Mrs. Franck paced in front of her husband's store at the corner of Myrtle Avenue and Pearl Street. In her arms she held her infant daughter who had been acting up inside the store, and she hoped the fresh air would have a calming effect on the baby. As she rocked the baby in her arms, Mrs. Franck noticed Albert Herrick enter his house at 339 Pearl Street. The Franck's and Herrick's had been neighbors and friends for a long time and when Mr. Herrick entered his home Mrs. Franck noted how well he looked and how neatly he was dressed, even though his wife was away in the country.

Mrs. Franck continued rocking the baby in her arms as she strolled down the street. When she reached a point directly in front of Herrick's basement door, she heard sounds she could not immediately identify coming from inside the house. Whether she heard a pistol shot or the sounds of a scuffle she could not tell, but whatever the noise was it made her nervous and impressed upon her mind that something awful had happened. She recognized Mr. Herrick's voice and believed she heard him trying to open the front basement door. An instant later, Herrick came out. He staggered from side to side and stumbled as he went up the three steps. In one of his hands was a lit candle. His face was covered with blood that flowed down until his shirt and other clothing were dyed with it. As he sunk to the ground Herrick feebly cried, "murder."

Despite Herrick's cry, as neighbors gathered around him the first thought was that Herrick had taken ill and injured himself. A girl named Katie Hayes, who worked for the Franck's, ran to the Washington Street police station for help.

Detective George Zundt had been in the station house on another case, and he rushed to the scene with two uniformed officers. It took Zundt's experienced eye but a moment to discover that Albert Herrick, instead of being ill, was dying, if not dead from a gunshot wound. A close examination revealed that Herrick had been shot just above the heart by what may have been a .32 caliber bullet.

When the body was removed, Zundt assessed the house. It was a three story and basement brick structure with a piazza running from the front stoop to the upper side of it and darkening the front basement. Zundt found the basement floor consisted of a front and back basement and a laundry. From the cellar steps to the front basement door were spots and pools of blood. He saw no evidence indicating a struggle and the walls were red stained as if hands covered with blood had been placed against them. Directly in the center of the basement door was a bullet hole. The bullet had penetrated the door, struck the wall that supported the stoop, against which it was flattened before falling to the ground. Detective Zundt found the bullet and placed it in his pocket. As he began making inquiries, Zundt found what seemed like hundreds of stories circulating through the streets. He very quickly found that most of these stories were created by the imaginations of those who told them.

Mr. Herrick had been in the liquor business at 60 William Street in New York, in partnership with A.D. Holbert. Herrick's wife left the city on July 11th to spend the summer in the country. The Herrick's had been married for ten years, but Mrs. Herrick had been previously married and had a twenty-year-old son named Thomas Armstrong. According to some neighbors, Mr. Herrick and Thomas Armstrong were the only occupants of the house, and Thomas worked as a driver for Wechsler & Abraham, Fulton Street dry goods dealers.

Detective Zundt took an immediate interest in Thomas Armstrong, especially when the young man could not be located, and his employer said he was currently on vacation. Zundt learned that Armstrong had relatives living in Hoboken, New Jersey, and he started off for that city after learning the location of the houses of three aunts and cousins. Thomas Armstrong was found at the home of his aunt, Mrs. Pierson.

Armstrong seemed more annoyed than nervous at Zundt's presence and after the detective explained why he was there, Armstrong said, "It's strange you should want me."

Zundt brought Armstrong back to Brooklyn where the young man insisted he had nothing to do with his stepfather's murder, and he seemed to be able to account for all his time on the day and evening of the killing. So convincing was Armstrong that some high-ranking police officials were theorizing that the murder was committed by a burglar who was surprised in the cellar by Mr. Herrick. Detective Zundt, however, discounted that theory and focused on Thomas Armstrong. Experience had taught Zundt that a thief caught in the house, while he might fire a shot at his discoverer to enable him to escape, would not follow him and fire another at a distance as was the case in this shooting. Two facts were sure. There was a bullet hole in the front basement door and Mr. Herrick was the only person to come out that door. That meant the shot that went through the door was fired from behind Herrick. Zundt was sure a burglar would not fire at a man who was running away. Another fact to discredit the burglar theory was that nothing was stolen from the house.

The investigation was becoming increasingly frustrating to Zundt. The more people he interviewed the more the stories regarding the relationship between Armstrong and Herrick differed. Some people said they had a relationship like a close father and son or like two brothers, but others said Armstrong was deathly afraid of his bigger, physically imposing stepfather. Zundt learned that Herrick had once beat a man senseless for talking to his wife without permission.

Zundt wasn't sure which stories were true until Mrs. Herrick returned from the country, and he finally had the opportunity to sit down with her. Mrs. Herrick said that Thomas was a good and affectionate boy and was very badly treated by her husband. She said that while she was in the country, Albert had written her a letter stating that when she returned, either he or Thomas would have to leave the house. Mrs. Herrick said that her husband never drank, but that he had a very violent temper, and she always feared he would do Tommy some serious harm. She shook her head when commenting that her husband could not get along with her son, and that her husband did not seem like he wanted to get along with Thomas. Mrs. Herrick said she could never believe that Thomas killed her husband in cold blood because he was just too kind to commit such an act.

Detective Zundt kept pressing Armstrong, but he kept denying having anything to do with the murder. After his talk with Mrs. Herrick, Zundt tried a different approach. He told Thomas that just because someone killed another person, it didn't necessarily make them a murderer. Armstrong was becoming emotional as Zundt spoke, and his emotions skyrocketed when the interview was interrupted by a visit from Armstrong's childhood friend, James Murphy. At first, Zundt was going to prevent the visit, but he decided to let the visit take place when he saw Armstrong's response.

Thomas completely broke down and cried like a baby. "Oh, Jimmy, you do not know how glad I am to see you. You are the only friend I have in the world. Will you stand by me?"

"Of course, I'll stand by you," Murphy pledged. "How did this happen, Tommy?" Murphy asked.

Armstrong looked at his friend, and then turned to Detective Zundt. Zundt nodded. "Go ahead, Thomas, it's time to tell us what happened."

Thomas gulped and turned back to Murphy. "When I left you Monday morning, I went to the house, but I was afraid to go in. I had had a big argument with my stepfather the day before and I wanted to avoid him, but I didn't know where to go. I went out to the park and then came back again, and my stepfather came to Stein's stable at about 8 o'clock, where he saw me and rushed at me. He cursed me, and if I hadn't skipped, he would have laid me out. I went back to the house after I thought he had gone to New York. I went up to the bedroom where me and the old man slept. I was searching the desk in the room for paper because I intended to write a letter to my stepfather to try to mend our relationship. Suddenly, the old man entered the bedroom and yelled, 'You son of a bitch, what are you doing here?' He rushed at me, and I jumped off the bed and grabbed the pistol that he always kept next to his bed. I was afraid to use it, though, and he rushed after me. I again jumped over the bed and ran downstairs into the cellar. He grabbed a lit candle and came after me in the cellar. I kept close to the wall and when he got down, I made a rush for the stairs. He made a grab for me at the top and I turned and fired one or two shots. I then ran to the back door, and I thought he was coming after me when I fired again. I fired in all four shots, three, I think when he was coming up the stairs and one when at the back door. I then got out the back way and went to Prospect Park and from there to Hoboken. I threw the pistol in the river because I was so excited that I could not think."

Armstrong was still tried for murder even though Zundt believed the confession he received made a strong argument for self-defense. At the trial, Armstrong's lawyer made a masterful defense based on self-defense and the jury acquitted Armstrong of murder. As he was leaving the courthouse flanked by his supporters, Armstrong locked eyes with a man leaning on a fence in front of the courthouse. George Zundt nodded and winked as Thomas Armstrong was swept away by his friends.[58]

There was one person involved with the case who was found guilty of a crime. Katie Hayes, the pretty servant girl who worked for Mrs. Franck who had been the first to give the alarm to the police that Mr. Herrick had been killed, was sentenced to 8-months in the penitentiary by Justice Walsh for stealing $20 worth of clothing and jewelry from Mrs. Franck.[59]

CHAPTER 26: STOP, OR I'LL SHOOT

At 9:30 A.M. Joseph Perry entered Martin Schneider's liquor store at the corner of Bond and Fulton Streets, and descended to the wine cellar, where he began to destroy what property he could find. Schneider tried to make him leave but Perry declined and then Schneider locked the store and went for a policeman. He returned with Detective Zundt. Together they went to the cellar, but Perry could not be found. Zundt drew his revolver and called, "Now I'm going to shoot him."

The warning had the desired effect, for Perry sprang up from behind a pile of rubbish, exclaiming, "For God's sake, don't shoot."

Perry had caused about $50 damage by cutting off the lead pipe from the ale pumps and was locked up. He told Justice Walsh that he did not know what he was doing, as he had taken a glass of beer on an empty stomach, and it had got the best of him. He pled guilty.[60]

CHAPTER 27: THE FAVORITE BROTHER-IN-LAW

Miss Tillie Hahn was a domestic employed by F. Ahlers, a saloon keeper at the corner of Court and Union Streets. According to Miss Hahn, she was alone in her employer's home, knitting in the kitchen, when the door was opened suddenly, and a masked burglar burst into the room. She said the crook then bound and gagged her before stealing $190 from the house and making his escape.

Police were suspicious that Tillie's story wasn't true, especially when Dr. Matheson, who was called in when the girl was found by Mrs. Ahlers and her mother-in-law, claimed that the girl had not been unconscious at any time during the night and that her bonds were not consistent with someone who had been securely tied up by another person.

Miss Tillie stuck her original statement, and it appeared that nothing could be done to shake her story. After two other detectives could make no headway on the case, George Zundt had a long talk with the girl, and secured an entirely new account of the alleged robbery. Tillie's story was a most peculiar one. She still stuck to the story of the robbery, but accused her sister's husband of being the thief, and contradicted herself in many ways. Nevertheless, her story led to the arrest of Joseph Kelly, of West 37th Street in New York.

Tillie said that her brother-in-law entered the home and told her he was going to rob the house and she made no resistance. Kelly had no revolver nor was he masked, as she first stated, and after he had taken possession of the money in Mrs. Ahler's trunk and was about to leave she submitted to being bound and gagged in order to give color to the story she first told of the robbery.

Kelly was arrested at his home by Zundt and brought to Brooklyn and locked up in the Butler Street police station. He told a completely different story. "I went home on Thursday night at the time the robbery was being committed. I don't know what has gotten into Tillie to tell such a lie. She has always been a truthful girl. I read about the robbery in Friday's papers, and I came over to Brooklyn to see her at the suggestion of my wife. Tillie told me all about the robbery and I sympathized with her. She told me a long story about the masked robber, and I don't see why she would accuse me. There is something else back of this and I hope that the girl will tell the truth. I never was arrested in my life, and to think of being accused by my sister-in-law whom I have always thought the world of -."

Kelly's story carried conviction with it. He was an old man of 60 years and would be the last one in the world to be selected as a man who would play the part of a masked burglar. In view of the story first told by Tillie Hahn and her subsequent confession to Zundt, it was only a question of who was telling the truth.[61]

Captain Leavey summoned Tillie to the police station and in the presence of several witnesses, got the girl to make a statement, which was taken down in writing. She adhered to the story that her brother-in-law had stolen $190 from Mrs. Ahlers' trunk, and that before he left, she submitted to be bound and gagged in order to make her story appear true. The statement was read to her, and she affixed her signature.

There was no doubt that Tillie, in accusing her brother -in-law, was trying to shield the real culprit. Zundt had learned something in addition to what had already been told. It was now known that some time ago Kelly called on Tillie and borrowed some money. Whether the girl took the amount from her own savings or helped herself to the money which belonged to her mistress was not known. The girl was aware of the fact that Mrs. Ahlers kept money in her trunk, a fact that was known to her and Mrs. Ahlers only.

Mrs. Ahlers stated that she had not seen the money in her trunk for three weeks, but that she had not looked to see if it was there. On Tuesday she told Tillie that she was going to overhaul the trunk, and right there came the motive for the alleged visit of the masked man. Tillie had probably been helping herself to Mrs. Ahlers' money, and when the latter gave notice of overhauling the trunk, the girl knew that the money would be missed, and she took the necessary steps to protect herself.

The way the girl was bound gave rise to the theory that she had tied herself. Her story that she was unconscious for nearly two hours was denied by Dr. Matheson, who said that he was ready to make an affidavit that the girl's senses had never left her. Kelly was arraigned before Justice Tighe and pleaded not guilty. Tillie was committed to jail as a witness.[62]

Detective Zundt was convinced that Tillie was not telling the whole truth, so he had her brought over to the detectives room from jail to keep pressing her for the true story. At first, she stuck to her story, but finally gave way under Zundt's persistent questioning. With the first show of emotion that her stoic features had betrayed since the robbery she began to weep and finally came clean about the whole affair.

"I stole the money myself," she said. No one assisted me and my brother-in-law, Joseph Kelly, is innocent. I don't know why I did it. Mrs. Ahlers was always kind to me during the time I was with her. I accused Joe to shield myself. On Thursday night after Mr. and Mrs. Ahlers and Mr. Ahlers mother started to the theatre, the thought came into my head that I could buy a good deal with the money which I knew was in Mrs. Ahlers' trunk. I took a lamp, went into Mrs. Ahlers' room, forced the hinges off the trunk and then took the money. To make the story of the robbery I intended to tell look stronger I took my own trunk and scattered the contents about the room. I knew they would not return until 11 o'clock, so I sat down and bound my limbs and then waited until I heard them entering the house. I put the rope, which I had already tied about my hands, placed the handkerchief in my mouth and then twisted my wrists until the rope was tight. Then I threw myself on the floor where I was found. I knew it would not do to keep the money about me, so as soon as I took it, I went to the woodshed in the yard and hid the money under a loose board in the floor. That is the true story."

Zundt took the girl to Mrs. Ahlers' house. She led him directly to the woodshed, lifted the board and taking from under it a small brown paper parcel, handed it to the detective. The parcel was opened and found to contain $190, all intact. Mrs. Ahlers was informed of the turn affairs had taken and was very glad to get her money back. Tillie would not look at her mistress and held her head in shame while in her presence.[63]

CHAPTER 28: SEVERANCE PAY

When William D. Lohman, ex-cashier of Brooklyn's Excise Department left his job with a lot of the city's money, Superintendent Campbell put Zundt on the case, and through his connection in Brooklyn's German community he developed information indicating that Lohman was in Toronto.

The Toronto Detective Department was advised that Lohman was in Toronto, and they were provided with a detailed description. A couple of Toronto officers noticed him in the rotunda of the Palmer House, and concluding he was the wanted man, approached him and asked his name. The man responded that he was John Rickard of New York. In answer to further questions the officers learned that he had been staying at the house about two months and had been quiet and unobtrusive in his demeanor and had not at any time spent money lavishly. In fact, after the first week of his stay, during which he paid regular commercial rates, he told Mr. Palmer he would be there for some time and got a special reduction on the rent. All these facts did not appear to indicate a successful thief, but still detectives believed they had the right man. They called him by his proper name, and he unhesitatingly responded. They told him their business and Lohman admitted his identity. He said he had been expecting it for some time and at once consented to walk down to police headquarters. When informed that he was being charged with embezzling $80,000, Lohman protested and said he only took $19,400. None of the money was found.

When Chief Constable Garner, of Toronto, notified Campbell of Lohman's capture, Detective Zundt was immediately dispatched to bring him back to Brooklyn.

Lohman was a very large man weighing in excess of three hundred pounds. For eight years he had been a cashier in the Excise Department and handled all the money from people applying for licenses. Lohman had been an ardent supporter of David Boody in his run for mayor, and he was particularly devastated when Boody lost. On January 27th Lohman left for a vacation in Philadephia where he had stated his intention to attend a meeting of a singing society, of which he was president. With the administration of the new mayor about to take their positions, outgoing Excise Commissioners Schilemann and Cahill confirmed that Lohman's accounts were alright at the time he departed for Philadelphia. Lohman never returned to work, and an audit of his accounts conducted by the new administration showed that he had stolen $19,400 in cash.[64]

By the time Detective Zundt returned to Brooklyn with Lohman, it was clear that the disgraced cashier was going to plead guilty and throw himself on the mercy of the court.

"How could he do otherwise?" Zundt commented. "During the trip from Canada he told me the whole story. He told me he gave the money to his old friend, Frank McCutheon to invest in the business of nickel operated horse racing machines. If he doesn't plead guilty, I will be a witness against him."

Lohman did plead guilty and was sentenced to seven years in prison. For Detective Zundt, the Lohman case was one of his most enjoyable assignments. He was treated royally by the Toronto police and could only hope for more assignments of that nature. It was hardly likely, however, that Zundt would do anymore traveling. Shortly after Lohman pled guilty Detective Zundt was assigned to permanent duty in the Fire Marshal's office. The purchase of fire insurance had grown greatly in the latter part of the 19th century, and with the increase in insurance came the increase in incidents of arson to fraudulently collect on these policies. There had been a great deal of these suspicious fires and insurance claims in Brooklyn, so it was decided to make a special effort to run down these offenders. Along with this assignment came a promotion for Zundt, who was elevated to the rank of Detective Sergeant.[65]

CHAPTER 29: DOUBLE TROUBLE

What started as a misunderstanding between three detectives quickly began to escalate to a point where it became a career threatening situation for George Zundt. The misunderstanding quickly escalated into a dispute because Inspector Mackellar, who was in charge of the detective squad, was on vacation and not present to straighten things out. The trouble began with an arrest made by Detective Sergeant Zundt and the disclosures that followed a search of the prisoner's pockets.

Fire Marshal Benjamin Lewis and Zundt appeared in Justice Walsh's court with Jacob Klein of 74 Johnson Avenue, and applied for a warrant for the arrest of John Weinig on a charge of having attempted to extort money by impersonating an official. The story was supplied by Mr. Klein, who swore that on June 30th there was a fire at his house and considerable damage was done. On July 2nd, he said Weinig visited him and represented that he was an assistant fire marshal. Weinig asked Klein if he was insured, received an affirmative reply and after looking over the charred apartment walked away promising to return soon. Klein said Weinig came back on July 6th and asked to be shown Klein's policy of insurance. He looked at it, handed it back and then startled Klein by saying, "I want a few dollars."

"For what?" asked Klein.

"I want $50. It is for the fire marshal, and if you do not give it to me, you will be arrested tomorrow," it was alleged Weinig replied.

"If the fire marshal wants to see me, he can summon me to his office," Mr. Klein responded before Weinig went away.

Klein later went to the office of Fire Marshal Lewis and revealed what Weinig had said. Mr. Lewis swore he had no assistant on the case and Justice Walsh issued the warrant. Mr. Lewis said that he had received several other complaints against Weinig, alleging that he had been carrying on an extensive business as a bogus assistant fire marshal. With warrant in hand, Zundt traveled to 100 Goerck Street in New

York, where Miss Woolf, Weinig's girlfriend, winked at the detective and said, "You can't get Weinig. You have a warrant for him, and we've had a tip."

Two days later Zundt found Weinig on the street near his place of employment. Back in Brooklyn, when Weinig was searched at the Adams Street police station, letters of recommendation written by Assistant Fire Marshal Freel of New York and Detective Sergeants Kelly and Ryan of Brooklyn were found on him. On the back of one of Ryan's business cards was a handwritten note:

The bearer, Mr. Weinig, is a good citizen and we recommend him to anyone who may see this.

Weinig was indignant over his arrest. He declared that he knew nothing at all about Klein and indicated that he was the victim of a plot to send him to prison. Weinig was a hatter by trade, of Austrian birth and was 29 years old.

Despite Kelly and Ryan's recommendations, Detective Zundt declared that Weinig's character was bad and that he had enough evidence to secure his conviction on the charge. Kelly and Ryan did not reach the boiling point in their indignation over the arrest, until they heard that Fire Marshal Lewis had been talking about their connection with the case as shady and had been alleging that there was an official leak somewhere. Mr. Lewis claimed that Weinig had received a tip about the existence of the warrant for his arrest from an official source.

"I don't care to talk about the case," said Kelly to a reporter, "until Inspector Mackellar returns to town. Our connection with the matter will be cleared up then, but for the present I'd prefer to keep quiet."

"I wouldn't prefer to keep quiet," raged Ryan. "Statements have been made about us that should be cleared up at once." Ryan then made several uncomplimentary remarks about Zundt before continuing his story. "This man Weinig is as straight as a string, as far as we know. He has been supplying Inspector Mackellar with valuable information in an attempt to break up a gang of firebugs who have been working in this city and in New York. He was introduced to Inspector Mackellar by Deputy Fire Marshal Freel of New York City, and I understand that he had been working against the gang in New York City, too. As far as we know he is a man of excellent character. I don't believe that he ever impersonated the fire marshal for the purpose of extorting money. My impression is that he can prove an alibi as far as the specification about extortion on July 6th is concerned, for I am almost sure that Mr. Kelly and I saw him in that hat factory where he works on that day. This may be a put up job to get rid of him, although, mind you, I don't say so. The gang has tried it before. On June 25th he was arrested in New York City for burglary. He was charged with having broken into Rabbi Friedmann's house and stolen a number of the clergyman's robes. When arraigned before Justice Hogan in New York there was no evidence against him and he at once was discharged. Since then, he says that men have been following him and he thinks that the firebugs mean to murder him or get rid of him in some way. The recommendation Mr. Kelly and I signed for him was written that he might have no trouble in securing a permit to carry a pistol. If Zundt had been so anxious to get Weinig he could have secured him before this. Weinig was in the detective office at headquarters speaking to Detective Sergeant Strong last Saturday. We never gave him a tip about the warrant."

"I don't know Klein, and never saw him in my life," said Weinig to a reporter. "It is true that I knew there was a warrant out for me, but I did not keep out of the way. I was talking to Detective Sergeant Strong at police headquarters on Saturday. This is a job put up on me by the gang and I can prove my innocence."

The prisoner was later arraigned before Justice Walsh and remanded until Friday morning for examination. Inspector Mackellar had commenced the prosecution against the firebugs without consultation with Fire Marshal Lewis and it was alleged there was a feeling of jealousy on account of the case. It was not likely, though, that Mr. Lewis knew of Weinig's connection with the prosecutions. Deputy

Police Commissioner Harmon said that Zundt was aware of Weinig's connection with the case.

"Just as soon as Inspector Mackellar returns," Mr. Harmon said, "we will have this matter investigated. Zundt knew all about Weining. I want to have the entire proceeding thoroughly sifted." [66]

Suddenly, Detective Zundt found himself in the middle of a very sticky situation. His new partners at the Fire Marshal's office insinuated that the Weinig case involved corruption across the river in New York, while the Brooklyn Police were livid about their operation against the firebug gang being upset, and they levied allegations of corruption against the Fire Marshal's office.

Brooklyn was seeing steady increases in the numbers of arson cases, and the fast developing rift between the police and the fire marshal was sure to delight all the firebugs in the country and bring them flocking to Brooklyn.[67]

The rift only deepened at Weinig's arraignment. "Can you reduce my bail?" Weinig asked.

"I seriously object to the bail being reduced," Mr. Lewis said. "Since this charge has been made, three or four other people have appeared at my office and desired to enter complaints against this man for trying to extort money from them."

"Your honor," an exasperated Weinig pled, "This is a put up job. I am innocent of the charge against me."

At that point, Deputy Fire Marshal Freel of New York stepped up and addressed Judge Tighe. "Your honor, while not being a lawyer, I would like to have something to say in reference to this case."

"I object to the Deputy Fire Marshal of New York appearing in this case," said Mr. Lewis, "unless he is a witness to the specific charge preferred against this man."

"But I ask to make the statement as a matter of courtesy," countered Freel.

"You may go on and make your statement," said the judge.

"This man Weinig," Freel began, "is a material witness against men who have been indicted by a grand jury in Brooklyn. In fact, he has been doing some work for the police of Kings County, with the knowledge of Superintendent Campbell and Inspector Mackellar. He is working hand in hand with the department."

"What is the object of these remarks?" asked the judge.

"Well, I think this case should be postponed until Inspector Mackellar returns from his vacation," replied Freel.

"But your honor, this man is a perfect stranger to me," said Mr. Lewis, looking at Freel. "He has no right to appear in this case."

"But there should be some courtesy shown to a representative from the metropolis," Freel shot back.

"We have lots of work today," said Justice Tighe, "and I will adjourn this case until Wednesday morning and at the same time reduce the bail from $1,500 to $500. I also say that I only want to examine the complaining witness." [68]

On Saturday morning, Inspector Mackellar arrived at police headquarters, fresh from a vacation in the woods of Maine, and was besieged by reporters asking about the Weinig case.

"I have not looked over the statements so far submitted," Mackellar said, "and there is a great deal of additional evidence which has not yet come out. It would be materially impossible for me at this time to pronounce an opinion as to the guilt or innocence of Mr. Weinig. All I know about him is that he was brought over here by the Assistant Fire Marshal of New York and introduced to the Superintendent. The Superintendent sent him to me, and I introduced him to the headquarters detectives, with whom he has since been working. He appeared to do good work, as we got a number of convictions of firebugs on evidence furnished or procured by him. George Zundt is now attached to fire headquarters and that is how he came to make the arrest."

Zundt was located by reporters at fire headquarters. "I only made the arrest in the case and I did not collect any evidence against this man Weinig. I do not know if there is a great deal of evidence against him."

Assistant Fire Marshal Rice was the person most aggrieved by Weinig's alleged misconduct, because he is the man Weinig allegedly impersonated. "This is not a fight between the police department and the fire department," Rice said. "My interest in the matter is to vindicate myself and to show that the department is clear of any extortionate practices. We are being blamed for getting a lot of money that we never got, and we want vindication. The evidence against Weinig is very considerable. The witnesses are in most instances his own countrymen, and there is some circumstantial evidence. On Friday, when we went to look for Weinig, we shadowed his girlfriend all day long, and in the evening, we went to her home and she put her finger to her nose and said, "You can't get Weinig. He got a tip that you have a warrant for him. If Weinig was innocent, would she act like that? We went away and did not turn up again for three days, when we got word where we could find Weinig. He knew there was a warrant out for him, and he acknowledged he had been in police headquarters on Saturday, the day after his girl told us we could not get him. Why did he not give himself up?" [69]

Anonymous members of the Brooklyn Police Department were critical of Zundt's actions in the case and hoped that the department took a very close look at all the circumstances connected with Zundt's arrest of a man, who while accused of a serious crime on one hand, was at the same time, for all intents and purposes enjoying the fullest confidence of several other officers and was in a measure supposed to be aiding them in their investigations. The feeling was that once Zundt had been detached to the fire department, he had forgotten that he was still a police detective and felt he could act independent of the police department. The result was a growing divide between Zundt and his former detective comrades. [70]

At his arraignment, Weinig made a complaint to Deputy Commissioner Harman that Detective Zundt had failed to return to him certain papers taken from him at the time of his arrest. These included a hatter's trade check, a letter of recommendation from Thomas Freel, Assistant Fire Marshal of New York, and other documents.[71]

While a grand jury was yet to hear the evidence against David Weinig, Police Commissioner Welles had taken a look at the mixed-up case and decided to prefer charges against Detective Zundt. The detective was accused of making his complaint against Weinig before the fire marshal instead of before the chief of police, as was his duty, as it was claimed, according to the rules of the department.

As things stood, it seemed that Inspector Mackellar's men had the best of the argument and that both the fire marshal and his detective assistant went very much out of their way to secure a case.[72]

When the grand jury convened and heard evidence that David Weinig was not even in Brooklyn at the time he was supposedly trying to extort money from Mr. Klein, they quickly discharged the case. Weinig was in the clear, but the problems were just beginning for Assistant Fire Commissioner Lewis and Detective Zundt.

The day after Weinig was set free, Benjamin Lewis retired, and on the afternoon of October 27th, had ex-Fire Marshal Lewis known what was going on in Brooklyn a little after noon, he would have breathed a huge sigh of relief as the Kaiser Wilhelm swung out of her dock and turned her nose down the bay on her long run to Europe, with Lewis and his wife safely on her deck. While Lewis was saying goodbye to his friends and seeing to the passing of his luggage, Justice Cullen, of the Supreme Court was signing an order for his arrest. The order was rushed into the hands of a deputy sheriff. But it was too late. The former Fire Marshal of Brooklyn had shaken the dust of Kings County from his feet and had gone over the river to board the steamer bound for Europe. Benjamin Lewis was gone, but George Zundt was very much alive and well in Brooklyn and was the subject of a similar warrant.

The warrant complained that Zundt had taken Weinig before the fire marshal for examination in violation of the rules of the department and had also failed to turn over to the property clerk certain articles which he took from the prisoner. Weinig had a lot of witnesses ready to testify, but Zundt brought the matter to a close by pleading guilty and receiving a reprimand from the police commissioner as punishment.[73]

With his guilty plea, George Zundt may have pulled himself out of the frying pan, but something going on in New York City was about to place him right back into the fire.

•••

Corruption and graft were rampant in the New York City Police Department in the 19th century. During 1894 and 1895 the Lexow Committee was a major New York State probe into police corruption in New York City. The Lexow Committee inquiry, which took its name from the committee's chairman, State Senator Clarence Lexow, was the widest ranging of several such commissions empaneled during the 19th century. The testimony collected during its hearings ran to over 10,000 pages and the resultant scandal played a major part in the defeat of Tammany Hall in the elections of 1894 and the election of the reform administration of Mayor William L. Strong. The Brooklyn Police Department had managed to steer clear of the daily sensational testimony until Charles M. Patterson began testifying.

The testimony given by Patterson in regard to Detective Zundt created quite a stir in police circles in Brooklyn. Mr. Patterson's story, as told before the committee, was that in June, 1893, he was robbed of a diamond stud on the Brooklyn Bridge Station platform of the Brooklyn elevated railroad. He notified the Brooklyn Police Department and Detectives Zundt and Mahoney were detailed to the case.

The next day Zundt called at Patterson's place of business in New York and told him he had located the stud in Lemon's Pawn Shop, on Sixth Avenue in Manhattan. Patterson said he went with the detective to the pawnshop, but instead of getting the stone from the pawnbroker, he said Zundt took it out of his own pocket and demanded $60 as the amount paid out by the pawnbroker, besides $50 which had been offered as a reward for the recovery of the gem. Patterson said he did not have the cash with him and offered a check for the amount to the pawnbroker. The pawnbroker refused the check and Zundt offered to advance the money on the check. Patterson then paid Zundt $50 reward for the recovery of the diamond, but on the advice of friends the next day, he stopped payment on the check, as he was advised he had been swindled. Patterson said he believed that the diamond pin had never been pawned, and that Zundt, the pawnbroker, and New York detectives colluded to swindle him out of $60.

Zundt had just finished dealing with the charges made by David Weinig, and now, Senator Bradley, of the Lexow Committee was calling upon Police Commissioner Welles, with an indignant attitude. He told the commissioner that the evidence before the Lexow Committee was a slap in the face to him. He had been standing up for the Brooklyn Police Department all through the New York investigation, and his feelings could be imagined when this testimony was given. Mr. Patterson had called Zundt a thief several times during the testimony, and the impression left on the minds of the committee was that Zundt was in collusion with the New York Detectives. Commissioner Welles told the senator that if Zundt were innocent, he would stand by him, but if guilty, the "Lord help him." [74]

As he got on in years, something strange seemed to be happening to George Zundt. It was some 23-years since he joined the force, and for more than twenty of those years he had a spotless record and never gave his enemies a chance to wag their heads at him – and he did have enemies. Some said Zundt possessed an aloof and abrasive personality, partly the product of the fact that despite the lengthy tenure of the veteran detective, in the insulated world of a department dominated by "Irish Cops," this moody German-speaking officer was in many ways, an outsider. His assignment to the Fire Marshal's office only served to exasperate his detachment from the police department. At a time when Zundt should have been thinking of retiring and enjoying a well-earned pension, he found himself under investigation, first through his arrest of David Weinig, and then through the allegations of Charles Patterson to the Lexow Committee. Whether or not his integrity had been compromised had not yet been determined. What was fact, however, was that Zundt had run afoul of some of his fellow detectives in connection with his work in the Fire Marshal's Office, and some within the department would take great joy in seeing Zundt take a fall through the allegations of Charles Patterson.[75]

There were times when George Zundt was his own worst enemy in providing ammunition to the anti-Zundt faction. Take, for example, a very strange case in 1883 that nearly spun out of control. On election day Zundt suggested to his colleagues at police headquarters that a pool of 25-cents from each person should be raised to be awarded to the person guessing nearest to the number of votes for the mayoral candidates. The idea was well received and almost everyone working in police headquarters participated, including the detectives, telegraph operators, the drill captain, policemen, captains, and reporters. Since the idea had originated with Zundt, it was thought proper that he should collect the money and pay the lucky winner. Zundt recorded every participant's guess and when the pool was closed at noon, he had collected $15.

When the results came in on election night it was clear that Mayor Low had defeated Mr. Hendrix. Early the next morning a very happy clerk named John Conesy jubilantly entered the detectives office and declared, "Hey, boss, I guess that pool belongs to me."

For some unknown reason, Zundt replied, "Oh, go about your business, will you. I've got no money that belongs to you."

"We'll see about that," Conesy sneered. "I guessed nearest on this election business – don't forget that, boss."

Detective Zundt refused to give up the money, though it was clear in his record of the pool that Conesy came nearest to the actual number of votes. Several other persons who were part of the pool, including some of his fellow detectives demanded that Zundt pay Conesy.

To all the demands Zundt replied, "I have got the money, and no power under heaven can make me give it up."

Finding it impossible to gain satisfaction, John Conesy reported the incident to Deputy Commissioner Langford, and asked that the matter be investigated. There was a rule in the police department that any officer not paying his debts could be brought to trial for conduct unbecoming an officer. Zundt was set to be put on trial before Commissioner Jourdan. His friends in the detective squad begged him to pay Conesy the money owed to him before the matter became a full-blown scandal. Finally, Zundt gave in and paid Conesy. It was never learned why Zundt had refused to pay the money.[76]

Another incident involved a dispute between Zundt and Detective Michael Powers, one of Zundt's main enemies, in which Zundt was accused of using insulting language about Powers on the steps of the Municipal Building. Police Commissioner Carroll, who had been appointed by incoming Mayor Whitney eight months earlier, looked at the complaint and noticed it was signed "Michael F. Powers, Acting Sergeant, Detective Squad." Carroll immediately took up an issue other than the complaint against Zundt.

"Who made you sergeant?" The commissioner asked

"I am not a sergeant," Powers replied.

"But you have signed yourself such. There is no such position in the department."

"Well," Powers shrugged, "The Superintendent so stated to me."

"He ought to communicate with me first," Carroll said. "You are in the office because it is necessary to have someone there all the time. You are not superior to any of your colleagues."

"Suppose I receive an order from the Superintendent," Powers challenged, "I have to give the order to the men."

"The Superintendent is very jealous of his power," Carroll shot back. "I wanted to give one of the inspectors charge of the detectives, but the Superintendent said no. I don't know what authority you think you were given."

"There is none," Powers stated.

"I don't think it is right for him or for you to assume power," Carroll said. "I didn't know there was such an office as Sergeant of

Detectives, and if there is I should have been notified. I am fresh here and like to know what is going on. There must be such an office before there can be a man in it."

Powers called Detective Thomas Shaughnessy, of the Myrtle Avenue station, as his witness against Zundt.

Shaughnessy said, "We were talking on the stoop and the question of bed bugs came up. Inspector McLaughlin said he couldn't stand those in the bed upstairs, and I said I had to tackle them because I can't sleep in a chair. Zundt said, 'Powers put the bed bugs in the bed.' That was all that was said at the time, and I took it as a joke. I told Powers about it not thinking he would come up here about it. I didn't think there was any disrespect in the remark."

Detective Powers asked Shaughnessy if he recalled while they were both in Duffy's Saloon that a man named Bray approached Powers and said Zundt had told him that Powers would commit an obscene act upon Superintendent Campbell if the Superintendent asked him to.

At that point Commissioner Carroll referred to the proceeding as nonsense and dismissed the charges.[77]

Despite the occasional strange behavior, Detective Zundt was known to be genial with most of his colleagues and acquaintances. But as his career drew nearer to its conclusion, many noticed that Zundt had become a victim to something closely resembling melancholia. He was described as walking around like a sick hen and talking like an undertaker in hard luck. It was quite possible that his sullen mood was the result of his ever-increasing weight. Zundt had always been a large man, but as he got older, he seemed to be getting rounder every day. This, very well, could have been the secret of his misery. He would regularly comment that he did not know what was going to become of him. He had walked, run, punched the bag, and at last, driven to extremity, had given up the use of beer, but all to no avail. He continued to grow and supposed after a while some museum man would get him and make him a "Fat Man" exhibit. [78]

George Zundt's weight became a secondary issue when the Patterson issue and his diamond pin continued to heat up. When the incident had occurred in June 1893, Superintendent Campbell had not considered the Patterson incident very serious, and he had originally treated it as such. But the Lexow Committee had thrown a spotlight on the case, and Campbell couldn't help but take notice when McManus and Lang, two New York detectives, were implicated in the case and reduced in rank by Superintendent Byrnes, of the New York Police Department.

When the case was fresh, Superintendent Campbell had ordered Detective Zundt to make a report of the case, which must have been satisfactory, as the matter was dropped and Zundt was advised by Campbell to sue Mr. Patterson civilly for the amount of the check Patterson had stopped payment on.

Strangely, this report of Zundt's could not be found among the archives of the police department. Campbell remembered receiving Zundt's report but didn't remember its contents, as it was a very lengthy document. How the report got lost was a mystery, and it was thought to have been burned with other old papers when the old administration left office.

At Campbell's direction, Zundt wrote another very long, detailed report on the incident.

Sir – It is a source of unfortunate sorrow to me to learn that the report which I made to the Department in the month of June 1893, relating to the loss of a diamond pin by Charles Patterson cannot be found in the archives of the Department. You will remember that I personally handed the report to you.

I supposed that the matter had been closed beyond resurrection because of the investigation made by the department at the time and have no doubt that you were under the same impression and handed the report to the commissioner of the department, and that he laid it aside instead of filing it, as is usually done in such cases. I believe it will yet be recovered, but I cannot wait for that time.

I regret that I did not retain a copy of the report, and now in compliance with your request I restate the facts: On the 6th of June 1893, between the hours of 6 and 7 P.M., Mr. Charles Patterson and a gentleman, introduced to me as Mr. Dick, called at the detective office of the department and reported the loss of a diamond pin while coming over the Brooklyn Bridge in the cars.

I was in the office at the time and was instructed by Inspector Reilly to note Patterson's statement, which I did. The following morning the loss was entered in the department blotter by Detective Strong, the clerk having charge of such matters. When Mr. Patterson called at the office, he gave a description of the person suspected and offered a reward of $50. (It should be noted that during this era policemen were allowed to accept rewards from citizens if the receipt of the reward was approved by the department)

He said he would pay all expenses incurred in the recovery of the pin and would make the person instrumental in arresting the thief a handsome present. The following morning, June 7th, Detective Mahoney and I went to Police Headquarters, New York, for the purpose of examining portraits in the Rogues' Gallery – could find no person that would lead to the identification of the person described. While Mahoney and I were there, Mr. Patterson came in and reported the robbery to the officer in charge. As Mahoney and I were leaving headquarters we met Detectives McManus and Lang, of New York. We related the facts to them, and they subsequently had charge of the matter in New York. We returned to Brooklyn, and about two or three days afterward I received a telegram from McManus making an appointment.

Mahoney and I saw him in the evening at the Brooklyn Bridge, Brooklyn side. He stated to us he believed the pin could be located and was under the impression it was pawned for $75, where he could not state. I subsequently received from him notice to meet him at the bridge.

He then stated that he believed he had the pin located, and he had received a pawn ticket for the pin through the mail. I asked him for the ticket. He said he did not have it with him. I asked him for the name of the pawn shop where the pin was. He refused to state it. He wanted me to go with him. I told him I would not go as I could not identify the pin but that I would notify Mr. Patterson by postal card, and I would meet him at his place of employment the next morning at 11 o'clock. Mahoney and I saw Mr. Patterson the next morning. Mr. Patterson could not go with us, then being too busy.

He requested me to wait. I waited and sent Mahoney to Sixth Avenue and Twenty-seventh street to notify Lang and McManus that I was detained. Mr. Patterson said he could not identify the pin positively, but he would take an employee of Austin Nichols & Co., from whom he bought the pin.

Patterson, the employee whose name I do not remember, and I went to Twenty-ninth Street and Sixth Avenue. Saw Lang, McManus, and Mahoney there on our arrival. Patterson wanted to know who those parties were. I explained. We then went to Lemon's pawnshop, Sixth Avenue near Twenty-ninth Street.

McManus or Lang had evidently been there, because the pawnbroker immediately produced the pin. Patterson could not positively identify the pin. The employee thought it was Mr. Patterson's pin. Patterson replied, "How do you know it is my pin?" He said, "Because I have the ticket, which I received through the mail. I do not know who sent it." Patterson wanted to take the pin to a jewelry store for further identification. The pawnbroker refused, saying it was pledged for $61.80. Mr. Patterson said, "I have no money with me at present. Here is my card. I represent Austin, Nichols & Co.

I'll give you a check for the amount." The broker refused to take the check. A few days previous I had been paid my salary. I had been at Austin Nichols & Co.'s, and saw that Mr. Patterson occupied a prominent position there.

I told Mr. Patterson that I would let him have the amount. He thanked me, accepted the amount and said he would give me a check later. Mr. Patterson paid $61.80 to the pawnbroker and took the pin on condition that if it were not his he might return it and receive the amount.

This the pawnbroker agreed to do. Mahoney, Patterson, and I went to Wark's Jewelry store, Barclay and Greenwich streets. They identified the pin as one sold by them to the employee of Austin Nichols & Co. Mr. Patterson, after the identification of the pin by the jeweler, wanted to leave and take the pin with him.

I told him I could not permit him to do so, as I had been sent on the matter by my superior, and it was my duty to take the pin to the property clerk. Mr. Patterson said he was too busy to go to Brooklyn and said he would give us $15 if we would let him have the pin, and my superior would know nothing about it.

The fifteen dollars I took to be a gift, and if I accepted it, he would also give me a check for $61.80, the amount I had advanced.

I asked him to show me the pin, which he did. This was the first time I had ever had the pin in my possession. McManus and Lang had been handling the matter up to the time we left the pawn shop, and Mr. Patterson had the pin in his possession until we got to the jewelry store.

I asked Mr. Patterson to let me see the pin so I could get possession of it and deliver it to the property clerk. I delivered it to the clerk, who turned it over to Mr. Patterson. Mr. Patterson, upon delivery of the pin, said, "Mr. Zundt, I want to pay you what I owe you." He drew two checks, one for $50, the reward, and one for $60 and handed them to me.

I said, "Mr. Patterson, the $50 reward does not belong to me, that goes to New York, to the men who located your property. There is $1.80 due me yet on the $60 check." He said, "That's alright. The check was made out, let the matter go." I applied for and received permission from the Commissioner of the department to receive the $50 check.

The next morning, I received a letter from Mr. Patterson, which letter I have in my possession, stating he had given me two checks, one for a $50 *reward, which he was duty bound to pay; the check for $60 he had stopped payment on.*

He had consulted counsel and was satisfied he was not liable for the amount, and that if I did not get the thief who stole the pin he would come over and lay the matter before Superintendent Campbell. On receipt of the letter, I saw Superintendent Campbell and asked him if I should answer it.

He said, "Yes." I answered it by telling Mr. Patterson I would only be too pleased to have him come over and lay the whole affair before Superintendent Campbell. I believe Mr. Patterson subsequently saw Superintendent Campbell.

Mr. Campbell told me to go to New York, that Mr. Patterson wanted to see me. I went to New York and saw Mr. Patterson. He stated to me that if I would go to a pawnbroker's and I could satisfy him and he could see the entry on the books, and the ticket, he would pay me the amount I had advanced him. I went with him, and he saw the entry in the books himself, took a note of it and the pawn ticket also.

Mr. Patterson apologized and said he would mail me a check in the morning enclosed in a complimentary letter, which he failed to do. I then took the letter stating he had stopped payment on the check and showed it to the Commissioner and asked him what I should do in the matter.

I told the Commissioner I had given him the money and I could not afford to lose it. He said the only thing I could do was to sue him for it. I then placed the matter in the hands of Wilbur & Devanny, my lawyers. The complaint in that suit was sworn to by me on the 23rd day of May 1894, before John H. Kyle.

The facts herein embodied were all placed before Superintendent Byrnes by Detective Mahoney and myself, soon after the occurrence, and Detective McManus and Lang were reduced to the ranks, as I was informed, by reason of the statement made by myself and Mahoney to Superintendent Byrnes.

George V. Zundt

Detective Sergeant

When the Commissioner had read Zundt's statement he said that he proposed to hear from the two New York officers and the pawnbroker before making a statement. "If there is any ground for charges being preferred against Zundt for his connection with the matter they certainly will." [79]

Officers McManus and Lang, of New York, called on Police Commissioner Welles and told him all about their connection with the recovery of Mr. Patterson's diamond pin. The two New York officers were with the commissioner for about half an hour, and when they had taken their departure, he was asked if he had anything to say in connection with the matter. He said that he would take considerable time to look over the statements and evidence and until he had done this, he would not dismiss the case. The New York officers denied many of the statements made by Zundt, and the commissioner intended to probe the matter to the bottom.[80]

Commissioner Welles finally decided that charges were warranted against Detective Zundt, but those praying for Zundt's downfall were disappointed when the charges Zundt was called upon to answer was that of failing to turn in to the pension fund 10 percent of the reward he received for recovering property.

Patterson testified and reiterated the story he told to the Lexow Committee, how he had to pay detectives in New York money for the recovery of his property who were in league with Brooklyn officers and a pawnbroker where his diamond pin was found in pawn.

Then came McManus with his story. The New York detective glanced at Zundt as he took the witness stand. He took a chew of gum from his mouth and nervously squeezed the sticky mess between his fingers as his examination proceeded.

McManus testified that he had received a letter from Zundt stating that a well-known Brooklynite, a good fellow and a friend of his, had lost his diamond pin in the elevated cars. He asked him to try to find it. McManus said he went to Simpson's and Lemon's, on Sixth Avenue, and made an appointment to meet Zundt and Mahoney. He sent a telegram but around the same time received another letter from Zundt asking him to come to Brooklyn with his partner Lang.

"We met Zundt and Mahoney at the entrance to the bridge," said McManus, "and I told him that I had seen several stones, some in Simpson's and the others in Lemon's that answered the description of the stolen property. When we mentioned Lemon's name Zundt said, 'By God, that must be the one,' at the same time pulling out a pawn ticket which he said someone sent him through the mail. I said alright to him and requested him to meet us on the New York side the following morning at which time we went to the pawnbroker's. There, Patterson wanted to give a check to redeem the stud, but the pawnbroker would not take it. Zundt then gave him the necessary amount and he handed Zundt a check to cover $60."

Once inside the pawn shop, McManus said they bid Zundt and Mahoney goodbye and that was the last he had seen of them until he was reduced in rank. He said he happened to meet Zundt one day and Zundt told him that Patterson had offered a $50 reward for the recovery of his property.

"Did you ever receive any money from Zundt or Mahoney?" the commissioner asked.

"Not a cent."

Lang also said he never received a cent from Zundt.

Mahoney said that Zundt told him Patterson was an old G.A.R. (Grand Army of the Republic) man and that he was going to recover his stolen pin at any cost. He detailed his visits to New York with Zundt and how the pin was recovered. He understood that the New York men got $5 apiece out of the reward, with which they were to purchase a hat. Mahoney said that the New York men told him they would take no part of the reward.

Zundt and Mahoney both swore that the $50 reward was offered to McManus and Lang at a meeting between the four detectives at Val Schmidt's saloon on Fulton Street. They both swore positively that McManus and his companion refused to take the money because the $61.80 check had been stopped and they asserted Zundt was entitled to the money. Then Zundt swore that he gave them each $5, the price of a hat, and Mahoney corroborated this story in so far that he had heard the price of a hat offered. Zundt indicated that Campbell had given him permission to break the rule and keep the reward. Mahoney said Zundt paid him $20.

McManus swore the pawn ticket had been sent to Zundt. Lang backed up McManus and said they were not even offered the $5 for a hat.[81] Francis Dallon, formerly deputy commissioner swore that he had been informed that the money was to be paid to New York detectives.

Commissioner Leonard Welles determined that Patterson's impression that the officers were guilty of collusion or in taking from him any money for division among themselves other than the $50 reward offered by him for the recovery of his stone, was incorrect. "The stone was pawned on June 13, 1893, by a man named Smith, who received a ticket for the same. The amount advanced was $60. On June 16th the stone was redeemed, and the ticket delivered to the pawnbroker. There had been no erasures or changes on the original entries in the books or the ticket. Much doubt existed as to who had the ticket. Detectives Zundt and Mahoney say Detective McManus, of New York, while McManus and Lang say it was Zundt. The pawnbroker knew he received the ticket but could not remember who gave it to him. Mr. Zundt advanced the money to redeem the stone, he said out of good feeling for Mr. Patterson, but I think the speedy possession of the reward was the motive. The evidence shows that Zundt had permission from the department to receive the reward, but the division of the same was made contrary to the statement made by Zundt when making the application. The testimony shows Zundt received $30 and Mahoney $20, the New York men getting nothing. As Mr. Patterson offered the reward and was present when the amount $61.80 was paid to the pawnbroker, and afterward gave the checks for the same, he was cognizant of the whole transaction. The officer, Mahoney, is now not in the department. Officer Zundt violated a rule of the department in not depositing 10 percent of the reward in the pension fund and is subject to discipline and punishment for the same." [82]

Zundt had told his story to Superintendent Byrnes over a year earlier, and on the strength of it Detectives McManus and Lang were sent back to posts as common patrolmen. Since the Lexow hearing and the subsequent developments, McManus was restored to the rank of detective.

Lang and McManus both wanted to see Zundt dismissed from the Brooklyn force. They claimed he swindled them out of their share of Patterson's reward and was one of the chief instruments of their official degradation.

Much to the chagrin of McManus, Lang, and the rest of the Zundt haters, Police Commissioner Welles dismissed the charges against George V. Zundt. Mr. Welles explained that in light of the testimony given by Francis Dallon formerly deputy police Commissioner, he had no alternative. Mr. Dallon swore that Zundt informed him of the fact that Charles Patterson had paid a reward of $50 for the recovery of the diamond stud and had represented that the reward properly belonged to the New York officers who had been instrumental in finding the property. Understanding that the money was to be paid to the New York Detectives Mr. Dallon testified that he said, "You can keep it."

The complaint against Zundt, Mr. Welles said, was effectively disposed of by this evidence. "I did not take into consideration the question of veracity between Zundt and Mahoney, who swore the reward had been offered to the New York men and McManus and

Lang, who testified that they had not been offered and had not received anything from the reward," said Mr. Welles. "That evidence really had nothing to do with the case when you looked into the matter. The simple fact was that Mr. Dallon had given Zundt permission to receive the reward without making the usual contribution to the pension fund on the ground that the money was to go to the New York men. Mr. Dallon was the recognized authority at the time, and I had no right to go behind his acts. That is why I dismissed the complaint against Zundt."

Despite the ill will existing between Zundt, and some members of his department, the detective was popular in the German community, and it was alleged that strong pressure was exerted on his behalf. He was a veteran of the war and a member of the Saengerbund Singing Society. But despite the outcome of his trial there was a distinct impression at police headquarters that Zundt had fallen a great many points in the estimation of Commissioner Welles. Zundt swore that he had not only offered the New York Detectives the reward, but when they refused it he gave them each $5 for a hat. McManus and Lang very distinctly swore that Mr. Zundt had not offered them a penny of reward at any time.[83]

Those dissatisfied with the outcome of the trial scoffed at its farcical nature, citing that the charge was of such a trivial and inconsequential character. They mocked at the expense of a trial just to determine how guilty Zundt was in retaining a few paltry dollars, which, as claimed, he should have turned over to the pension fund. A great many people believed that it mattered very little what became of this "rake off" of $5 or so, and that Commissioner Welles had adroitly sidestepped what should have been the main issue of the trial, and that was whether or not Patterson had been swindled out of a sum of money by a combination of New York and Brooklyn detectives. That point, however, was the particular point to which no attention was paid. Instead, the trial addressed some flimsy infraction of the rules.

What people wanted to know was whether Zundt and others had got together and illegally levied a heavy assessment on a citizen for doing just what the city paid them well for, and nothing more. Anyone who listened to the evidence could not help thinking of the saying concerning the mountain and the mole hill.

As a source of amusement, the trial owed much in the way in which Zundt and McManus behaved themselves while it was going on. They were objects of mutual and special hate to one another, and the glances of contempt and scorn which they exchanged were enough to wither any ordinarily thin-skinned mortal. And how they sniffed and laughed in hollow mockery when their chance came. The trial was full of conflicting and contradictory testimony, but one fact was indisputable and left unresolved - somebody lied.[84]

CHAPTER 30: GONE BUT NOT FORGOTTEN

George Zundt retired on March 1, 1895, after spending 24-years on the job. For the past two years he had been assigned to the Fire Marshal's office. His pension was $850. [85]

His last two years on the job, especially his deteriorating relationship with some detectives, as well as the charges he had faced had only served to sour Zundt's opinion of the police department. When he handed in his retirement papers and departed police headquarters for the final time, there was no boisterous celebration, or line of well-wishers slapping his back and shaking his hand. Zundt placed his Grand Army hat on the back of his head and stated to a reporter in three separate languages that he would find a warm corner somewhere in this big world. He had made a pretty fair living and had no fear for the future.

Zundt possessed artistic talent, and over the years he had adorned the walls inside headquarters with his paintings. As soon as he could, he caused all the pictures belonging to him, which comprised almost all the pictures hanging in police headquarters, to be loosened from their places and carried to his home. The next thing that was heard about Mr. Zundt was that he had made a deal with Ex-Detective Mahoney. They pooled their resources and brains and started Zundt & Mahoney, Private Detectives.[86]

Before George Zundt could find that warm corner somewhere in this big world, he was forced to deal with some ghosts from his past. Jacob Klein and David Weinig were back.

Jacob Klein had been arrested in Philadelphia and was under indictment on a charge of arson. Klein was the man who had gone to Fire Marshal Lewis and Detective Zundt and alleged that David Weinig had attempted to extort money from him by impersonating an assistant fire marshal. These allegations led to Zundt's arrest of Weinig and a rupture between Zundt and the Central Office detectives who were using Weinig to aid them in ferreting out firebugs. The charge against Weinig was proved to be groundless, and since then he had been instrumental in convicting a number of New York firebugs, who were now in prison.

Klein was now being sought for the same June 30, 1894 incident from which he said Weinig had tried to extort him. Klein left Brooklyn after his indictment, and Weinig had been on the lookout for him. He learned that Klein was in Philadelphia a few days earlier and secured a warrant for his arrest.

Klein was arrested by Detective Sergeant Ryan. It was charged that on June 30, 1894, Klein set fire to his tailor shop at 74 Johnson Avenue for the purpose of securing a portion of the insurance carried on some of the furniture and fittings in the place. It was in this proceeding that Adolph Hirshkopf was said to have figured as the furnisher of the substances used to start the fire and other fires elsewhere.

After Klein was returned to Brooklyn and was questioned by District Attorney Backus, The D.A. declared that he would have some startling developments in the Klein firebug case. This declaration proved to be true when the grand jury returned indictments for conspiracy against ex-Fire Marshal Benjamin Lewis, ex Assistant Fire Marshal Rice, who served under Lewis, George Zundt, and Adolph Hirschkopf, who was in the tombs prison on a charge of murder in the first degree.

It may be recalled that Lewis, then Fire Marshal, Rice, and Zundt, started an investigation of the case even when Klein suddenly disappeared to parts unknown. Detective Sergeant Ryan had done some good work on the Klein case and much of his information was gained from Weinig. The success of Ryan was not pleasant to Zundt, and it was said that a good deal of professional jealousy was aroused by Ryan's work. But when the charge was heard before Justice Tighe Detective Ryan swore that at the very time Zundt charged Weinig with demanding the hush money of Klein, he and Weining were together watching Hirshkopf's house in New York. No indictment was ever returned against Weinig and when his case came up, he was discharged on his own recognizance.

It was out of that proceeding in the Weinig case that the present indictments of conspiracy against Lewis, Zundt and Rice were found. The allegation was understood to be that they conspired together to deprive Weinig of his liberty. The evidence as to the conspiracy to railroad Weinig to jail would have been incomplete had it not been for the testimony of Detectives Kelly and Ryan who testified that at the time Klein swore that Weinig was attempting to extort money from him, they had positive knowledge he was elsewhere. Klein swore that Weinig had visited him on July 2 and 6 1894. On July 2nd it was verified that Weinig was at work all day at Prentice's hat factory and on the 6th he was with Kelly and Ryan all day watching in front of Adolph Hirshkopf's residence at 128 Willet Street, New York, waiting for Meyer Brunner and Schler Rosenblum, for whom the detectives had warrants. At the time of Weinig's arrest, a bitter feeling arose between Ryan and Zundt and they had never forgiven each other since.

As soon as the grand jury returned the indictments in the county court, Judge Aspinall issued bench warrants and the detectives were hurried out to find the defendants.[87]

There was a rumor around town that Zundt had died suddenly and that his death was due to the excitement following his arrest, which took place late in the afternoon after the warrant was issued. Inquiry at his house happily led to a denial of the story. Mrs. Zundt said that her husband could not be seen but that he was feeling comfortable and confident. He was perfectly easy in his mind, she said, as to the outcome of the present proceedings.[88]

Three months after the indictment, Brooklyn was getting ready for the trial of ex-Detective Zundt, and the anti-Zundters were anticipating the celebration of his final downfall. Then, in a shocking move, District Attorney Backus moved before Judge Hurd in the county court for the dismissal of the charges against Lewis, Zundt, and

Rice. He said the reason for the application was that he did not feel confident of obtaining a conviction without the testimony of a witness who was ill. Zundt was said to have declared that he would not permit the motion to dismiss the indictment against him to be made without a protest. He had been held up as a lawbreaker and would insist on a trial to prove his innocence. Hurd granted the motion to dismiss anyway.[89]

George Zundt never really got a chance to enjoy himself in that small corner of the world. His health was beginning to fail, and he eventually had to give up his private investigation business in the Arbuckle Building in Manhattan.

Ever since he joined the fire department at the age of fourteen, Zundt always considered himself a "fire laddie." He spent a lot of his time relaxing in the exempt firemen rooms in the basement of City Hall. Zundt was suffering from Bright's Disease, an archaic term for what is now referred to as 'nephritis' - an inflammation of the kidneys, caused by toxins, infection or autoimmune conditions. On November 6, 1897, Zundt was in the firemen room when he became ill. An ambulance was called and he was taken to his home at 226 Schermerhorn Street. Zundt had been in poor health for some time.[90]

George Zundt died at his home on November 23, 1897, after a lingering illness. He was 52-years old. Zundt was one of Brooklyn's most well-known police officers and one of its greatest detectives.

Thirty-eight days after George Zundt died, the Brooklyn Police Department also passed away. On January 1, 1898, Brooklyn was absorbed into the newly consolidated Greater City of New York, depositing the Brooklyn Police Department into the ash heap of history.

When the Metropolitan Police Act was abolished in 1870, Brooklyn established an independent police department that functioned until the 1898 consolidation. George Zundt joined the

Brooklyn Police Department in 1871 and died in 1897. It seems fitting that Zundt was around for almost the entire golden age of Brooklyn policing, establishing himself as the Brooklyn Sleuth, and the greatest detective no one ever heard of.

George V. Zundt.

RUBENSTEIN CURSING DETECTIVE ZUNDT.
"You have brought me to the Gallows.   My blood shall haunt you around the world!"

CAPTAIN WADDY ARRESTING GONZALES.—(PHOTOGRAPHED BY WILLIAMSON, BROOKLYN, L. I.)

PATRICK CAMPBELL,
Superintendent of the Brooklyn Police.

JOHN MACKELLAR,
Inspector.

BIBLIOGRAPHY

1. The Brooklyn Daily Eagle, 8/27/1882, p1
2. William E.S. Fales, Brooklyn's Guardians, New York, 1887, p30
3. POLICE! POLICE!, Brooklyn Union, 5/15/1871
4. William E.S. Fales, Brooklyn's Guardians, New York, 1887, p42-58
5. The Brooklyn Daily Eagle, 2/1/1876, p4
6. The Times Union, 8/11/1871, p3
7. The Brooklyn Daily Eagle, 2/28/1872, p3
8. The Brooklyn Union, 5/28/1872, p2
9. The Times Union, 6/4/1874, p3
10. The Brooklyn Sunday Sun, 8/30/1874, p1
11. The Brooklyn Union, 7/23/1875, p1
12. The Brooklyn Daily Eagle, 7/22/1877, p1
13. William E.S. Fales, Brooklyn's Guardians, New York, 1887, p21
14. The Brooklyn Daily Eagle, 4/17/1892, p13
15. The Brooklyn Daily Eagle, 6/3/1877, p2
16. The Brooklyn Daily Eagle, 5/2/1886, p11
17. The Brooklyn Daily Eagle, 12/18/1877, p4
18. The Brooklyn Daily Eagle, 12/15/1875, p4
19. The Brooklyn Daily Eagle, 12/20/1875, p4
20. The Brooklyn Daily Eagle, 7/22/1877, p1
21. The Brooklyn Union, 5/9/1876, p4
22. The Brooklyn Daily Eagle, 2/14/1876, p4
23. The Brooklyn Daily Eagle, 5/10/1876, p4
24. The Brooklyn Daily Eagle, 2/11/1877, p4
25. The Brooklyn Daily Eagle, 1/6/1880, p3
26. The Times Union, 7/18/1883, p2
27. The Brooklyn Daily Eagle, 5/5/1887, p6

28. The Brooklyn Citizen, 1/8/1892, p5
29. The Brooklyn Daily Eagle, 8/7/1876, p4
30. The Brooklyn Daily Eagle, 3/2/1876, p4
31. The Brooklyn Daily Eagle, 3/6/1876, p4
32. The Brooklyn Daily Eagle, 5/24/1876, p4
33. Zarrillo, John, Brooklynology, 4/15/2014
34. The Brooklyn Daily Eagle, 6/6/1876, p4
35. The Brooklyn Daily Eagle, 7/5/1876, p4
36. The Brooklyn Daily Eagle, 8/3/1876, p4
37. The Brooklyn Daily Eagle, 8/16/1876, p4
38. The Brooklyn Daily Eagle, 12/30/1876, p4
39. The Brooklyn Daily Eagle, 12/30/1876, p4
40. Brooklyn Daily Eagle, 11/7/1876, p2
41. The Times Union, 3/12/1877, p6
42. The Brooklyn Union, 3/12/1877, p4
43. The Brooklyn Union, 3/12/1877, p4
44. The Brooklyn Daily Eagle, 6/8/1877, p4
45. The Brooklyn Daily Eagle, 9/7/1877, p4
46. The Brooklyn Daily Eagle, 9/7/1878, p4
47. The Brooklyn Daily Eagle, 11/10/1878, p4
48. The Brooklyn Daily Eagle, 11/13/1878, p4
49. The Brooklyn Daily Eagle, 10/6/1879, p4
50. Kings County Rural Gazette, 10/11/1879, p2
51. The Times Union, 10/8/1879, p4
52. The Brooklyn Daily Eagle, 11/14/1880, p4
53. The Brooklyn Daily Eagle, 12/6/1880, p2
54. The Brooklyn Union, 1/4/1881, p4
55. The Brooklyn Union, 7/21/1882, p4
56. The Brooklyn Daily eagle, 1/19/1884, p4
57. The Brooklyn Union, 12/26/1884, p1
58. The Brooklyn Union, 8/11/1885, p1
59. The Brooklyn Union, 8/20/1885, p5

60. The Times Union, 6/24/1890, p4
61. The Brooklyn Daily Eagle, 2/22/1891, p20
62. The Brooklyn Daily Eagle, 2/23/1891, p4
63. The Brooklyn Citizen, 2/25/1891, p1
64. The Brooklyn Daily Eagle, 4/23/1894, p1
65. The Brooklyn Daily Eagle, 4/29/1894, p2
66. The Brooklyn Daily Eagle, 7/25/1894, p10
67. The Brooklyn Daily Eagle, 7/26/1894, p4
68. The Brooklyn Citizen, 7/27/1894, p2
69. The Brooklyn Daily Eagle, 7/28/1894, p10
70. The Brooklyn Daily Eagle, 7/29/1894, p9
71. The Brooklyn Daily Eagle, 8/1/1894, p10
72. The Brooklyn Daily Eagle, 8/5/1894, p9
73. The Brooklyn Daily Eagle, 12/18.1894, p1
74. The Standard Union, 9/13/1894, p1
75. The Brooklyn Daily Eagle, 9/23/1894, p21
76. The Brooklyn Daily Eagle, 11/9/1883, p4
77. The Brooklyn Union, 8/3/1886, p1
78. The Brooklyn Daily Eagle, 4/10/1887, p4
79. The Brooklyn Citizen, 9/15/1894, p2
80. The Brooklyn Citizen, 9/18/1894, p1
81. The Brooklyn Daily Eagle, 10/16/1894, p12
82. The Brooklyn Citizen, 10/5/1894, p2
83. The Brooklyn Daily eagle, 10/17/1894, p12
84. The Brooklyn Daily Eagle, 10/21/1894, p22
85. The Standard Union, 3/1/1895, p1
86. The Brooklyn Daily Eagle, 3/13/1895, p5
87. The Brooklyn Daily Eagle, 3/13/1896, p1
88. The Brooklyn Daily Eagle, 3/14/1896, p1
89. The Brooklyn Daily Eagle, 6/29/1896, p2
90. The Brooklyn Daily Eagle, 11/7/1897, p1